PEARLS FALLS FAST

A Pearls Before Swine Treasury
Stephan Pastis

Andrews McMeel
Publishing®

Kansas City · Sydney · London

Other *Pearls Before Swine* Collections

Rat's Wars
Unsportsmanlike Conduct
Because Sometimes You Just Gotta Draw a Cover with Your Left Hand
Larry in Wonderland
When Pigs Fly
50,000,000 Pearls Fans Can't Be Wrong
The Saturday Evening Pearls
Macho Macho Animals
The Sopratos
Da Brudderhood of Zeeba Zeeba Eata
The Ratvolution Will Not Be Televised
Nighthogs
This Little Piggy Stayed Home
BLTs Taste So Darn Good

Treasuries

Pearls Freaks the #%# Out*
Pearls Blows Up
Pearls Sells Out
The Crass Menagerie
Lions and Tigers and Crocs, Oh My!
Sgt. Piggy's Lonely Hearts Club Comic

Gift Book

Da Crockydile Book o' Frendsheep

AMP! Comics for Kids

Beginning Pearls

Pearls Before Swine is distributed internationally by Universal Uclick.

Pearls Falls Fast copyright © 2014 by Stephan Pastis. All rights reserved. Printed in China. No part of this book may be used or reproduced in any manner whatsoever without written permission except in the case of reprints in the context of reviews.

Andrews McMeel Publishing, LLC
an Andrews McMeel Universal company
1130 Walnut Street, Kansas City, Missouri 64106

www.andrewsmcmeel.com

14 15 16 17 18 SDB 10 9 8 7 6 5 4 3 2 1

ISBN: 978-1-4494-4659-8

Library of Congress Control Number: 2013944239

Pearls Before Swine can be viewed on the internet at www.pearlscomic.com

These strips appeared in newspapers from February 28, 2011, to September 2, 2012.

Cover design: Tim Lynch
Photography: Thomas Gibson
Model: Jessica Poole
Image composite: Graphics Four
Assistant: Travis Garwood

ATTENTION: SCHOOLS AND BUSINESSES
Andrews McMeel books are available at quantity discounts with bulk purchase for educational, business, or sales promotional use. For information, please e-mail the Andrews McMeel Publishing Special Sales Department: specialsales@amuniversal.com

Dedication

To Dorothy O'Brien and Tim Lynch, without whose patience and brilliance these books would not be possible.

Introduction

My pen deserved better.

It had been with me for the better part of forty *Pearls* strips, roughly four weeks of drawing. And it was out of ink.

So I tossed it in the trash can.

But it seemed wrong.

Because for weeks, that pen had been my only friend. My only companion. Tonto to my Lone Ranger.

So I picked it up out of the trash can and held it high overhead. High enough that all the other pens in the pen tray could see it.

"This was a great pen," I declared in a brief, but moving eulogy.

A eulogy I said aloud so that the other pens could hear.

Then I held the pen close to my face.

"Well done," I said to it.

And with that, I set it down softly in the trash can.

I felt the ceremony was a critical counterbalance to the way I had treated one of the pen's compatriots.

For just months earlier, one of my pen's brethren had behaved badly, dropping a big glob of ink into the center of a near-finished *Pearls* strip.

"ARRRRRRRGGGGHHH," I yelled.

But that accomplished nothing. I needed to turn this negative into a positive.

So I lifted the bad pen high.

And WHAM.

I brought my arm swiftly down, smashing the pen nib into the hard wood surface of my drawing desk.

The nib was destroyed. Flattened like a boxer's broken nose.

"You see that?" I yelled to the other pens in the pen tray. "That's what will happen to you if you act like that."

None of the other pens said a word.

And sure enough, in the months that followed, all of my pens behaved well.

They were scared straight.

Stephan Pastis
March, 2014

Panel 1:
- HEY, L'IL GUARD DUCK, WHATEVER HAPPENED TO THOSE GOPHERS YOU TRAINED TO CARRY GRENADES?

Panel 2:
- I POINTED THEM TOWARD THE TALIBAN, BUT SOMEHOW THEY NEVER GOT FARTHER THAN PITTSBURGH. SO NOW I JUST USE THEM AROUND THE NEIGHBORHOOD FOR LITTLE DOMESTIC THINGS.
- LIKE WHAT?

Panel 3:
- MOW YOUR LAWN OR ELSE, BOB.

There's no better way to start off this commentary than with grenade-carrying gophers.

Panel 4:
- HEY, L'IL GUARD DUCK, ONE OF OUR NEIGHBORS JUST TOLD ME HE WAS THREATENED BY ONE OF YOUR GRENADE-CARRYING GOPHERS.
- THAT CAN'T BE, SIR. I HAVE TO APPROVE ALL HIGH-VALUE TARGETS.

Panel 5:
- WELL, IT HAPPENED.
- MERCY ME. THAT WOULD MEAN THAT MEMBERS OF MY GOPHER GRENADE BRIGADE HAVE GONE ROGUE. GOD ONLY KNOWS WHAT MILITARY OPERATIONS A UNIT LIKE THAT MIGHT COMMENCE.

Panel 6:
- TWO FREE HOT DOGS PLEASE.
- MARLBOR
- QUICKEE CONVENIENCE STORE

Notice how cleverly I didn't quite say "Marlboro" on that cigarette display, thus keeping me just outside the reach of trademark-infringement lawyers. So for the record, those are "Marlborf" cigarettes back there.

Panel 7:
- L'IL GUARD DUCK! REPORTS OF YOUR GOPHER GRENADE BRIGADE ARE POPPING UP EVERYWHERE!

Panel 8:
- I REALIZE THAT, SIR. I'M TRYING TO ASSESS THEIR INDIVIDUAL THREAT LEVELS BY DETERMINING WHICH ONES HAVE ADVANCED GRENADE TRAINING AND WHICH ONES ARE ONLY AT THE INTERMEDIATE LEVEL.
- WHAT'S THE DIFFERENCE?

Panel 9:
- HEY! I GOT THE PIN OUT!
- OOOH. IT'S SO SHINY.

Big, puffed-out lips are always good comedy.

7

Panel 1:
BAD NEWS, SIR, THE GOPHER GRENADE BRIGADE IS NOWHERE TO BE FOUND. MY BEST GUESS IS THEY'VE CROSSED THE BORDER INTO PAKISTAN.

PAKISTAN? WE'RE NOT ON THE BORDER OF PAKISTAN.

Panel 2:
THEN MY BEST GUESS IS THAT SOMEONE HERE IS GIVING THEM SAFE HAVEN.

WHO'S GOT ANY USE FOR A BUNCH OF GOPHERS WITH GRENADES?

Panel 3:
Sweet dreams, assasseen frends.

For those of you out there with grenades, I don't think it's recommended practice to go to sleep with them in your hands.

Panel 1:
HEY, ZEBRA...DID YOU EVER GET RID OF THAT DOGGY DOOR YOU HAVE IN YOUR BACK DOOR?

I WAS GOING TO, BECAUSE I DIDN'T WANT THE CROCS TO USE IT, BUT IT TURNS OUT THEY'RE TOO FAT TO SQUEEZE THROUGH.

Panel 2:
SO NOW WHAT?

SO NOW I JUST LEAVE IT... BELIEVE ME, WITH ALL THE PREDATORS AFTER ME, IT'S NICE TO HAVE AT LEAST ONE ENTRANCE TO THE HOUSE I DON'T HAVE TO WORRY ABOUT.

Panel 3:
NICE PAD.

Zebra's comment in the first panel harkens back to a strip about six years prior where the crocodiles got stuck trying to get through the doggy door.

Panel 1:
HEY, ZEBRA, I'M GOING TO THE KITCHEN...DO YOU WANT ANY—

Panel 2:
THE GOPHER GRENADE BRIGADE! WHAT ARE YOU DOING AT ZEBRA'S HOUSE?

WE ARE TRAINED ASSASSINS. WE ARE EFFICIENT. WE ARE DEADLY. AND WE ARE HERE TO BLOW UP YOUR FRIEND.

Panel 3:
OHH, THAT WOULD NOT BE VERY NICE. YOU TWO SHOULD LEAVE RIGHT NOW.

Panel 4:
FOR ASSASSINS, WE'RE PRETTY EASILY PERSUADED.

HEY, RAT, MIND PASSING THE SALT?
SINCE WHEN DO YOU LIKE GREASY FOOD?
SINCE I'VE BEEN DEPRESSED... IT MAKES ME FEEL BETTER.
WHAT ARE YOU DEPRESSED ABOUT?
I DUNNO. I JUST FEEL SO WORTHLESS. I FEEL LIKE I NEED TO TRANSFORM MY LIFE...YOU KNOW, BE THE GUY WHO FOUNDS AN ORPHANAGE, OR OPENS A FOOD BANK, OR CARES FOR THE SICK.
YOU SHOULD THINK ABOUT IT, TOO, RAT... YOU KNOW, THINK ABOUT SOMETHING GREAT AND MEANINGFUL YOU CAN DO FOR OTHERS.
I'LL PASS THE SALT.
GREAT.
HEY, RAT, WOULD YOU MIND PASSING THE —
HEY! ONE @#%@#☆ FAVOR A DAY, FATTY!!

I drew this little image of the panicked gopher in my sketchbook and just liked the way it looked, so I drew a strip around it.

I'm sort of ashamed that it took me ten years of doing *Pearls* to make my first dung beetle strip.

Who says you can't get a big ball of poop onto the comics page?

I have a Jewish friend who writes to me just before Yom Kippur to apologize for all the things she may have done wrong that year. It got me to thinking what Rat might do if he had to apologize for all the things he did wrong in a given year. And thus, this strip was born.

Beetle Bailey really did get a postage stamp. Which raises a lot of existential questions. Like, if there really is a God, how could he have let *Beetle Bailey* get a postage stamp?

Panel 1: Zeeba neighba...Look out weendow. Ees thundering hoofs of hundred zeeba migrating cross Serengeti. Come outside...Join you peeple...

Panel 2: Hoof Hoof Hoof Hoof Hoof Hoof

Panel 3: You drawings not dat photo-realistic, Larry. / Hey. Zeeba hoofs no go 'HOOF HOOF,' Bob.

Sadly, the crocs' drawing of a zebra is not much worse than my drawing of a zebra.

Panel 4: Hey, son, want feesh wid me and Bob? Lake s'pose have huge feesh. / WHAT ARE YOU GUYS USING FOR BAIT?

Panel 5: Bob.

Panel 6: You made me miss feesh.

But darn it, that's one heckuva well-drawn fish.

Panel 7: HEY, RAT, I'D LIKE YOU TO MEET SOME PEOPLE. THEY'RE **HUGE** FANS OF YOURS. / THEY REALLY, REALLY LIKE ME?

Panel 8: WELL, I WOULDN'T GO THAT FAR. THEY THINK YOU'RE OKAY. / YOU JUST SAID THEY'RE HUGE FANS.

Panel 9: I PREFER THE TERM 'PORTLY.' / SORRY. THEY'RE *PORTLY* FANS. / PARDON ME WHILE I BEAT THE PORTLY PIG. / HEY, DUDE. WE LIKE YOU, BUT NOT A LOT.

I've noticed that no one is just a "fan" of anything anymore. They either have to call themselves a "big fan" or a "huge fan." I'm not a huge fan of that.

Panel 1:
Pig: PIG?...IT'S ME, RAT...I CAN'T SLEEP...I'M TOO AFRAID.
Rat: AFRAID OF THE DARK?

Panel 2:
Pig: AFRAID OF LAZY CARTOONISTS WHO USE DARK ROOM GAGS TO SAVE THEMSELVES TWO PANELS OF DRAWING.

Panel 3:
Pig: THAT HURTS.

Whenever you see a week of strips where there is a blackout in a comic strip, you know that the cartoonist was going on vacation and had to bang out an extra week of strips that week.

Panel 1:
Pig: HEY, STEPH, YOU WENT TO THE UNIVERSITY OF CALIFORNIA AT BERKELEY, RIGHT?
Steph: YEP. I'M A CAL BEAR FOR LIFE.

Panel 2:
Pig: AND DOES YOUR SCHOOL HAVE A RIVAL CALLED...UHH......STANFORD?
Steph: YEP. WE CAN'T STAND 'EM. WHY?

Panel 3:
Pig: NO REASON.
Steph: TAKE IT OFF.
Stanford mascot: PIPE DOWN, SAD PUBLIC SCHOOL HIPPIE BOY.

You haven't experienced life until you've attended a Cal/Stanford football game and watched a drunk Oski the Bear (Cal's mascot) physically assault the Stanford Tree.

Panel 1:
Goat: WHAT ARE YOU WRITING, PIG?
Pig: GAME SHOW CONCEPTS...SEE, I'VE BEEN WATCHING THIS SHOW CALLED "MINUTE TO WIN IT," WHICH HAS THESE CHALLENGES YOU HAVE TO ACCOMPLISH IN A MINUTE, SO I THOUGHT, WHY NOT DO THE SAME THING, BUT SET IT IN A BATHROOM?

Panel 2:
Goat: I SEE...AND WHAT DO YOU HAVE IN MIND?
Pig: "HOUR TO SHOWER."

Panel 3:
Goat: UH...I DON'T THINK—
Pig: OKAY OKAY OKAY HOW 'BOUT "DAY TO GO POT*TAY*."

Random trivia: The host of *Minute to Win It*, celebrity chef Guy Fieri, is from my hometown of Santa Rosa, California. Our kids once played on the same soccer team. And I know what you're saying: "Fascinating!"

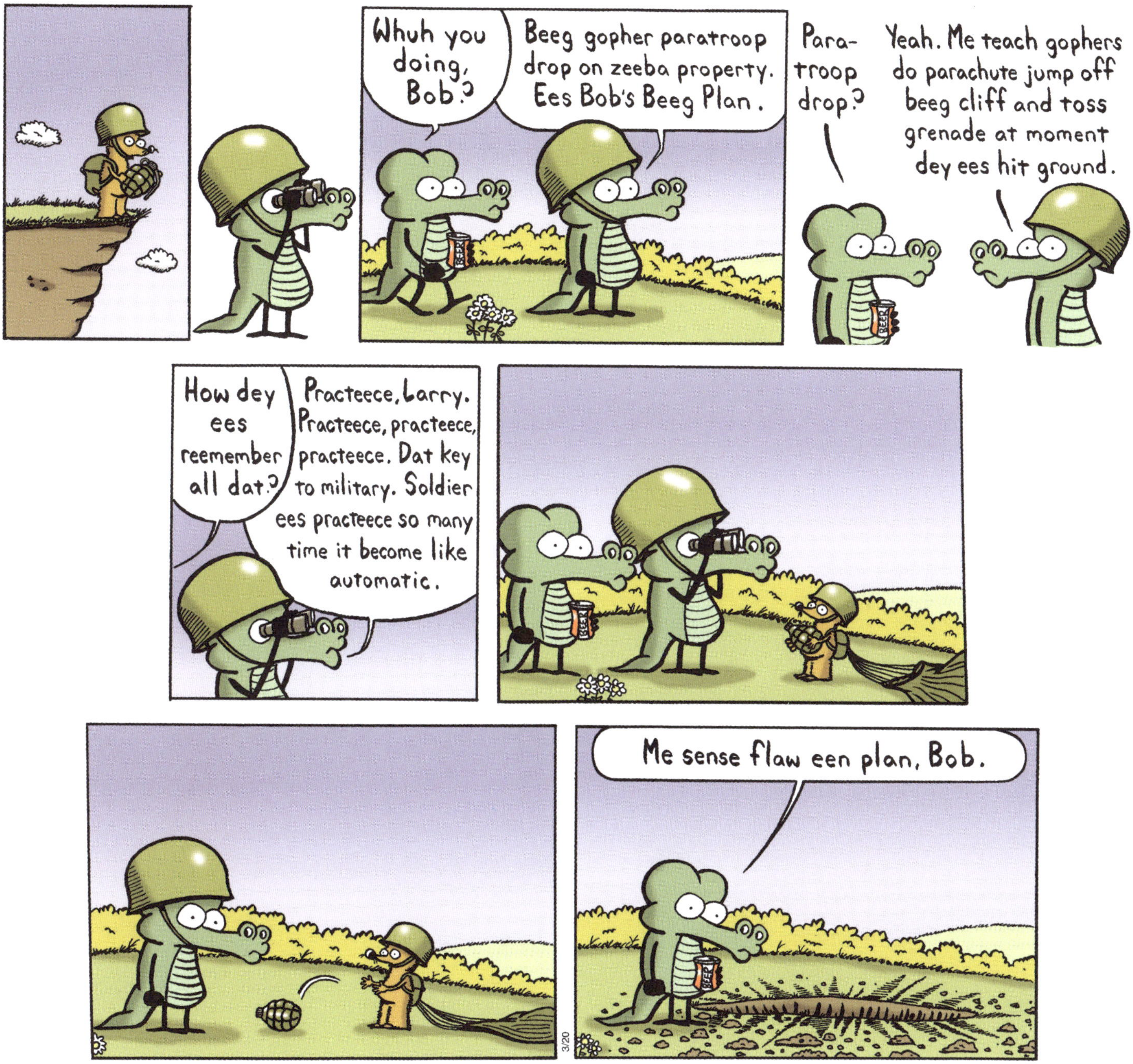
Whuh you doing, Bob?
Beeg gopher paratroop drop on zeeba property. Ees Bob's Beeg Plan.
Para-troop drop?
Yeah. Me teach gophers do parachute jump off beeg cliff and toss grenade at moment dey ees hit ground.
How dey ees reemember all dat?
Practeece, Larry. Practeece, practeece, practeece. Dat key to military. Soldier ees practeece so many time it become like automatic.
Me sense flaw een plan, Bob.

I was talking on the phone when I drew this strip and the lack of attention caused me to completely screw up the third panel. I drew Pig on the left and Goat on the right. This is a mistake because the third panel is drawn from a reverse perspective (i.e., it's viewed from *in front* of the diner counter, as opposed to behind). Rather than redraw the whole panel, I just took the image and reversed it on the computer. It may not be noticeable to you, but to me, both Goat and Pig look very odd in that panel—especially the shape of Pig's head. I think this is the first and only time I have reversed an image digitally in a *Pearls* strip.

So if you're one of those people out there who has never even used a pay phone, I'm here to tell you that you didn't miss much. It always smelled funny in there.

That is one well-drawn Superman. It's a wonder DC Comics hasn't called and asked me to do it full-time.

This strip was inspired by the old MTV show *Cribs*, where famous people would give you a tour of their home. Inevitably, whenever they got to their bedroom they would always say, "This is where the magic happens."

Okay, that's supposed to be that Monopoly guy. Please tell me you recognized him.

"Chowderhead" is a great and underutilized insult. So go out and call someone a chowderhead.

Panel 1 (3/28):

"HEY, RAT, HAVE YOU MET MY FRIEND, SMOKEY THE BEAR?"
"ONLY YOU CAN PREVENT FOREST FIRES."
"HE'D PROBABLY LIKE IT IF YOU BOUGHT HIM A BEER."
"WHY SHOULD I BUY HIM A BEER?"
"ONLY YOU CAN PREVENT SMOKEY GOING HOME SOBER."
"THIS COULD GET ANNOYING."
"ONLY YOU CAN PREVENT SMOKEY GOING HOME LONELY."
"CREEP."

Okay, two notes on this one. First, after it appeared, a number of people wrote to tell me that the bear's name is actually "Smokey Bear," not "Smokey *the* Bear." Second, it triggered a letter from someone at the U.S. Forest Service informing me that I was infringing on their trademark. Little did I know how protective they were of good ol' Smokey. In fact, if you're ever bored, look up "Smokey Bear Guidelines" on the internet. It's a whole list of rules for Smokey, including a section on how to properly wear the Smokey Bear costume. My favorite was Rule 9: "Do not use alcohol or illicit drugs prior to and during the Smokey Bear appearance."

Panel 2 (3/29):

"Whuh you reading, Bob?"
"Ees book on how crocs keel prey with death roll."
"Roll keel dem?"
"Oh, yeah. It snap neck. Why?"
"Peese. Eet wid dinner."

Thankfully, the Pillsbury Doughboy lawyers did not say a word. Apparently, they have a better sense of humor than the U.S. Forest Service.

Panel 3 (3/30):

"FOUND THE FAT MAN!"
"SOME PEOPLE WATCH ALFRED HITCHCOCK MOVIES FOR MORE THAN JUST SPOTTING THE ALFRED HITCHCOCK CAMEOS."
"OFF TO RENT MORE."

My son Thomas and I watched a number of Alfred Hitchcock films together, always trying to spot Hitchcock's appearance (for those that may not know, he was a director, but he generally tried to put himself in at least one scene in every film). The hardest movie for us to spot him in was *Rope*.

I've never understood why "chopped liver" is the universally understood term for something that no one values. Poor chopped liver.

In case you're not aware, there are some comics on the comics page that are nothing more than repeats (i.e., the exact same strips repeated over and over). The rerunning of strips is perhaps the single most destructive practice on the American comics page. For one thing, it takes away a younger artist's ability to get his comic strip onto the page. That's because a new comic can only go onto the page if another one first leaves. Traditionally, this happened when an artist died or retired. Now, such an event no longer necessarily means the end of the artist's strip. Also, the practice is totally unnecessary. If you want to read a strip that has already run in newspapers, simply buy the book collections.

Some time after this strip ran, I got an e-mail from my actual ninth-grade English teacher. It turns out she reads the strip. No word on whether she enjoys it.

Every once in a while, Rat's old girlfriend Farina makes an appearance. She is a germaphobe and hence lives in a protective bubble. But she goes so long between appearances that when she does appear, most people have no idea who she is. So I'm sure it triggers countless breakfast table discussions that go something like this:

Husband: "Honey, why's that pig in a bubble?" **Wife:** "Who knows? I prefer *The Family Circus*."

Panel 1 (strip 1):
- PIG GETS A VISIT FROM HIS HEAT-PACKING SEA ANEMONE ENEMY
- PLEASE DON'T AIM AT ME, ANNIE MAY, MY SEA ANEMONE ENEMY, AND BRING ABOUT THE END OF ME.

Panel 2:
- IT IS NOT I, YOUR SEA ANEMONE ENEMY, YOU SHOULD FEAR, PIG. IT IS A SEABIRD WHOSE ONLY GOAL WAS TO BRING A DAYTIME TALK SHOW TO WATCH HER PERFORM 'LA BOHEME' AT A GRAND OLE COUNTRY MUSIC VENUE.

Panel 3:
- THE OPRAH OPERA AT THE OPRY OSPREY?
- GREETINGS.
- GIVE ME THE GUN. I'LL SHOOT HIM MYSELF.

If you think the pun was hard to come up with, try drawing an osprey in a dress.

Strip 2, Panel 1:
- WHERE'S YOUR SEA ANEMONE ENEMY AND THE OPRAH OPERA AT THE OPRY OSPREY?
- THEY WENT HOME.

Panel 2:
- GOOD. YOU MEAN WE'RE DONE WITH ALL THAT STUPID WORDPLAY?
- YEAH. THE OSPREY HAD TO TAKE CARE OF HER SICK SON, OLLIE. I GUESS HE'S LOST ALL FEELING IN HIS WINGS. PLUS, HER TWO GIRLS, MOLLY AND ANNA, ARE TOO YOUNG TO TAKE CARE OF THEMSELVES. IT'S WEIRD 'CAUSE IT'S THE ONLY TIME EVER MY ENEMIES HAVE LEFT WITHOUT EVEN *TRYING* TO ATTACK.
- THAT'S QUITE AN ANOMALY.

Panel 3:
- WHAT'S AN ANOMALY?
- THE ANNA, MOLLY AND NUMB OLLIE ANOMALY.

Any time you see a character with ten lines of dialogue in one panel, you know that there is a very painful pun just around the corner.

Strip 3, Panel 1:
- DO YOU REALIZE THAT THE HUMAN HAND CONTAINS MORE GERMS THAN THE HUMAN MOUTH?
- SO?

Panel 2:
- SO WHAT DO WE DO WHEN WE GREET EACH OTHER? WE GRAB HANDS! FROM A HYGIENE PERSPECTIVE, WE MIGHT AS WELL KISS PEOPLE WE MEET ON THE MOUTH!

Panel 3: (hearts)

Panel 4:
- HOW DO YOU DO?

Think about this the next time you grab a handrail on a bus.

HEY, ZEBRA... WHATCHA WATCHING? / **FUNERAL... FOR ONE OF THE CROCS.**	**I DIDN'T THINK THEY HELD FUNERALS.** / **I DIDN'T EITHER... AT LEAST I'VE NEVER SEEN ONE.**
ME NEITHER. / **YEAH, AND IT'S WEIRD, BUT THERE'S SOMETHING ABOUT IT THAT'S REASSURING.**	**HOW SO?** / **I DUNNO. I GUESS IT MAKES ME REALIZE THAT THEY, TOO, SUFFER LOSS... THAT THEY, TOO, NEED THE COMFORT OF CEREMONY AND THE COMPANY OF LOVED ONES TO GET THEM THROUGH...I MEAN, LOOK, THEY'RE EVEN EULOGIZING HIM...**
Fred died. No one cares. Me take his beer.	**NEVER MIND.** / Hey... Why YOU geet his beer, Larry? / Because me beeger den you, Bob. / Okay... Me vote we keel Larry.

One of the only times I think I've ever drawn the crocs from behind. Oh, the artistic skills I have in my toolkit.

Panel 1:
- **Rat:** DO YOU REALIZE THAT IF YOU WERE TO GO INTO THE MEN'S ROOM OF THE SMALLEST BAR IN THE TINIEST TOWN IN AMERICA AND WRITE SOMETHING JUST ABOVE THE URINAL, YOU'D PROBABLY GET AT LEAST THREE PEOPLE TO READ IT?
- **Pig:** YEAH, SO?

Panel 2:
- **Rat:** SO THAT'S THREE MORE PEOPLE THAN READ GOAT'S BLOG.

Panel 3:
- **Goat:** PLEASE GO AWAY.
- **Rat:** HERE... FIND A RESTROOM.
- **Pig:** OH, GOAT, YOUR FIRST BIG BREAK!

I recently went drinking at various bars in Milwaukee, and found myself drawing my characters on the walls of at least three bathrooms. I also started drawing on a trash can on the way home. So somewhere, someone in Milwaukee sees Rat every time they take out their garbage.

Panel 4:
- **Pig:** ONE IS FILLED WITH SUGAR. ONE IS FILLED WITH ARROWS. ONE IS FILLED WITH SUGAR. ONE IS FILLED WITH ARROWS.

Panel 5:
- **Goat:** WHAT ARE YOU DOING, PIG?
- **Pig:** TRYING TO MEMORIZE THE DIFFERENCE BETWEEN CUSTARD AND CUSTER.

Panel 6:
- **Pig:** NOW YOU'VE THROWN ME OFF.

Panel 7:
- **Rat:** HEY THERE, GOAT...I'D LIKE YOU TO MEET MY FRIEND, BIG GUIDO.....YOU SHOULD KNOW, IF NEED BE, HE CAN HAVE YOU TAKEN CARE OF.

Panel 8:
- **Goat:** AAAHHHHHHHH

Panel 9:
- **Rat:** HE'S A NURSE.
- **Pig:** SOME CULTURAL STEREOTYPES ARE SO DARN PERVASIVE.

Having gotten complaint letters from Italian-American groups over my giving of Italian names to gangsters, I thought I'd do it again here, and then surprise them by making him a nurse.

I really don't like the use of fonts in comic strips. It looks too perfect.

I wonder how many plates I've drawn in *Pearls* over the years. It has to be in the thousands.

A world of infinite possibilities awaits you.	A world of ~~infinite~~ possibilities awaits you.
A world of ~~infinite~~ possibilities ~~awaits you~~ will one day await you.	A world of ~~infinite~~ possibilities ~~awaits you will~~ might one day await you.
A world ~~of infinite possibilities awaits you will~~ might one day await you.	~~A world of infinite possibilities awaits you will might one day await you.~~

You're hosed.

IT'S GETTING HARDER AND HARDER TO WRITE A COLLEGE GRADUATION CARD.

27

Strip 1 (4/18):

Panel 1:
— WHERE'S RAT TODAY?
— FLYING TO MAUI...HE CASHED IN SOME MILES FROM HIS CREDIT CARD AND GOT A FIRST CLASS TICKET.

Panel 2:
— RAT FLYING FIRST CLASS, HUH? HOPE IT DOESN'T GO TO HIS HEAD AND MAKE HIM FEEL ALL SUPERIOR TO THE PEOPLE IN COACH.
— HOW DO YOU MEAN?

Panel 3:
— AND IF THERE'S AN ACCIDENT, DO YOU BOTHER SAVING THE LITTLE PEOPLE?

I know what you're thinking. . . . Why does the plane appear to only have one seat? Answer: Because those chairs are a pain-in-the-@$$ to draw.

Strip 2 (4/19):

Panel 1:
— WHAT ARE YOU LOOKING AT, GOAT?
— HEY, PIG, MAYBE YOU CAN HELP ME...I'M TRYING TO PICK A VIVARIUM. I'M GONNA BUY A SNAKE AND I NEED A PLACE FOR HIM TO LIVE.

Panel 2:
— THEN WHY A VIVARIUM?
— BECAUSE IT'S WHERE YOU KEEP SNAKES.

Panel 3:
— I THOUGHT IT'S WHERE YOU KEPT VIVIANS.

Panel 4:
— MAYBE I DON'T NEED YOUR HELP.
— OHHHH, MY AUNT VIVIAN WOULD NEVER FIT IN THIS.

When I was a lawyer for a couple of years in Berkeley, California, our building was next door to a vivarium. I'm not quite sure which building had more snakes.

Strip 3 (4/20):

Panel 1:
— HEY, RAT, YOU MEETING ME AT THE DINER TODAY OR NOT?
— CAN'T. I'M GOING ON A HOLY CRUSADE AGAINST 'STARBUCKS.' THEY NEVER GIVE ME ENOUGH ROOM IN MY CUP FOR CREAM.

Panel 2:
— RAT, THE HOLY CRUSADES INVOLVED A BUNCH OF KNIGHTS IN THE MIDDLE AGES WHO TRIED TO RE-CLAIM THE HOLY LAND FOR CHRISTIANITY. I HARDLY THINK IT'S AN APT TERM FOR SOMEONE TRYING TO GET MORE ROOM IN HIS CUP FOR CREAM.

Panel 3:
— WHATEVER.
(shield reads: MORE ROOMETH)

Strip 1:

- "WHAT ARE YOU READING, GOAT?"
- "'THE IDIOT,' BY FYODOR DOSTOEVSKY."
- "THAT'S TOO BAD."
- "WHAT'S TOO BAD?"
- "SOMEONE STOLE THE TITLE OF YOUR AUTOBIOGRAPHY."
- "PLEASE GO AWAY."
- "IS 'MY SAD, LONELY LIFE' STILL AVAILABLE?"

I actually read *The Idiot*. I'd like that thirty hours of my life refunded.

Strip 2:

- "LET'S HAVE AN 'UGLY FACE' CONTEST TO SEE WHO CAN MAKE THE UGLIEST FACE."
- "WHOA. YOU WIN."
- "PLEASE GO AWAY."
- "DUDE, STOP. THE CONTEST IS OVER."

I play this game all the time with family members.

Strip 3:

- "YOU ENTER THIS WORLD ALONE. YOU LEAVE THIS WORLD ALONE."
- "BUT IN BETWEEN WE'VE GOT DONUTS!!"
- "IN BETWEEN, WE'VE GOT MORONS."
- "MMMMMMMM.... EXISTENCE GOOOOOOOOD."

| I AM NOT A GOOD CARTOONIST. | I AM NOT SMART. | I AM NOT FUNNY. | I AM NOT EVEN AMUSING. | TRUTH BE KNOWN, I SHOULD HAVE REMAINED AN ATTORNEY, WHICH IS WHAT I WAS BEFORE THIS JOB. |
| SO I'M SORRY FOR EVERYTHING. | I'M SORRY FOR THE POOR DRAWING. | I'M SORRY FOR MY ARROGANCE. | I'M SORRY FOR THE PUNS. | AND I'M SORRY FOR THE DISRESPECT I SHOWED TOWARD OTHER CARTOONISTS. |

BUT MOST OF ALL, I'M SORRY FOR HAVING AN UGLY, UGLY FACE.

NEW HOBBY?

PLEASE, SIR... NO HECKLING THE VENTRILOQUIST.

WHOA! WHICH ONE'S THE *REAL* DUMMY?

Conveniently, my goatee hid the lines that you would otherwise see on either side of a ventriloquist dummy's moveable mouth. Without that, I wouldn't have been able to do the joke, because you would know from the first panel that that was a dummy there.

Strip 1:

"Hullo. Me Eester Bunny. Me want hide eggs een you house."

"YEAH, WELL, THE EASTER BUNNY I KNOW DOESN'T NEED TO ARTIFICIALLY BUILD UP HIS COURAGE TO KNOCK ON MY DOOR PRETENDING HE'S THE EASTER BUNNY."

"It been tough year for Eester Bunnies."

Strip 2:

"DUDE, I THOUGHT YOU SAID YOU HAD A JOB INTERVIEW."

"I DO, BUT I LIKE THE COMFORT OF MY WARM COVERS."

"YEAH, WELL, EMPLOYERS LIKE PEOPLE WHO SHOW UP ON TIME."

"YEAH. YOU'RE RIGHT."

"AM I ON TIME?"

Strip 3:

"DUDE, CHECK IT... I'VE INVENTED A NEW EXPRESSION... IT'S, 'YO. SNAP. WHASSA MATTA HAMMA.?'"

"WHAT THE HECK'S THAT S'POSED TO MEAN?"

"IT MEANS, 'I JUST BURNED YOU. WHAT ARE YOU GONNA DO ABOUT IT?'... I'M HOPING IT SWEEPS THE NATION."

"I WOULDN'T LET IT SWEEP MY BATHROOM FLOOR."

"YO! SNAP! WHASSA MATTA HAMMA?!"

"IT'S A SAD DAY WHEN A NERD CARTOONIST GETS THE BETTER OF YOU."

Confession time: In my real life, I actually go around using this expression, in the vague hope that it will catch on. It's a little sad.

Strip 1:

- "HEY, THERE, GOAT.... I HEAR YOU'RE DATING SOMEONE."
- "YEAH...SHE'S SMART...TALL...SHE HAS BLUE EYES...AND SHE'S A DIRTY BLONDE."
- *SLAP*
- "I FELT COMPELLED TO DEFEND HER HONOR."

Strip 2:

- "HEY, RAT, IT'S ME AND GOAT...WE JUST THOUGHT WE'D CALL AND SEE WHAT YOU'RE DOING."
- "RIGHT NOW I'M WATCHING 'JERSEY SHORE,' AND UPDATING MY FACEBOOK PAGE AND FRYING A LITTLE BACON."
- "I THOUGHT YOU HAD TO DRIVE SOMEWHERE TODAY."
- "I'M DOING THAT, TOO."
- "THAT CAN'T BE SAFE."

I'm not sure too many people fry bacon while they drive, but still, you get the idea.

Strip 3:

- "HEY, PIG, CAN I DROP YOU INTO A CAGE OF ANGRY, HYPER-TERRITORIAL BABOONS?"
- "NO."
- "COULD I AT LEAST BORROW TEN DOLLARS?"
- "SURE."
- "THE KEY TO NEGOTIATION IS TO START BIG."

I wasn't a lawyer for ten years for nothing.

I think the crocs were supposed to be actually ringing the doorbell in that first panel, but I forgot and drew them as you see. So rather than redo the whole first panel, I just had one of the crocs say, "Ding dong ding dong."

Strip 1:

- WHERE WERE YOU THIS MORNING?
- FILLING OUT MY CALENDAR FOR THE MONTH. I LIKE TO KEEP ON TOP OF MY SOCIAL SCHEDULE.
- OH, YEAH? WHAT EVENTS DO YOU HAVE COMING UP?
- NEXT TUESDAY IS THE EXPIRATION DATE ON MY MILK.
- YOU MIGHT WANT TO GET OUT MORE.
- WHOA... SAME DAY AS THE CHEESE... GONNA BE A BUSY TUESDAY.

Strip 2:

- HEY, RAT, CHECK OUT THIS MODEL OF AN ATOLL I MADE... WHEN I PRESS THE BUTTON, IT SAYS STUFF... WATCH....
- I'm a ring of coral encircling a lagoon.
- HMM. THAT'S PRETTY COOL. LET ME TRY.
- You are a G*#@#$* idiot.
- OH MY GOODNESS.
- IF YOU CAN'T SAY SOMETHING NICE, DON'T SAY ANYTHING, ATOLL.
- DON'T YOU HAVE A FREEWAY YOU CAN PLAY ON?

I don't actually play on freeways.

Strip 3:

- WELL, GOAT, I SHOULD GO. I'VE GOT A BIG DATE TONIGHT.
- WELL, GOOD FOR YOU, PIG. YOU SURE SEEM TO HAVE GOTTEN OVER PIGITA. WHO'S THE NEW LADY?
- I'M THINKING YOU COULD DO BETTER.

She's not that bad looking for a girl composed of a mop, a pillow, and a garden hose.

Panel 1:
YOU KNOW, PIG, BEFORE YOU START DATING A MOP, YOU SHOULD TRY ONE OF THOSE INTERNET DATING SITES. YOU TELL THEM STUFF ABOUT YOURSELF, LIKE YOUR INTERESTS AND YOUR INTELLECT, AND THEY SUGGEST A GOOD MATE FOR YOU.

I TRIED THAT.

Panel 2:
WHO'D THEY SUGGEST?

A MOP.

Panel 3:
IT WAS LOVE AT FIRST SIGHT.

I have never actually tried an internet dating site. I think my wife would find it odd.

Panel 1:
WELL, GUYS, I BROKE UP WITH HOSANNA. SHE NEVER DID HAVE MUCH OF A PERSONALITY. SO NOW I'M DATING SOMEONE MORE CHARISMATIC. SOMEONE WHO REALLY LIGHTS UP A ROOM.

WELL, GOOD FOR YOU, PIG.. I'D LIKE TO MEET HER SOME DAY.

Panel 3:
AND TO THINK SOME CARTOONISTS TAKE PRIDE IN THEIR WORK.

Panel 1:
Humanity now stands rudderless. Hence, let us cry without cessation for the next thousand years.

Panel 2:
HEY, RAT. WHAT'S THAT YOU WROTE THERE?

MY FUTURE EULOGY.

Panel 3:
I'LL BE LEAVING NOW.

IS A THOUSAND YEARS TOO SHORT?

The greatest funeral quote ever was by Stan Laurel (of "Laurel and Hardy" fame), who once said to his friends, "If any of you cry at my funeral, I'll never speak to you again."

Crap. I just noticed a mistake in this one. I'll let you try to find it yourself.

Strip 1:

Panel 1: THE STUPID STATE WANTS TO RAISE MONEY BY EXPANDING THE STATE LOTTERY. NOW PEOPLE WILL SPEND MORE OF THEIR HARD-EARNED MONEY CHASING IMPOSSIBLE ODDS. / YEAH. THAT'S WHAT'S SO GREAT ABOUT THE LOTTERY.

Panel 2: WHY DOES THAT MAKE THE LOTTERY GREAT? / IT'S A TAX ON PEOPLE WHO CAN'T DO MATH.

Panel 3: PLEASE LEAVE ME ALONE. / NOW IF WE COULD JUST TAX GENERAL STUPIDITY. / FOUR LOTTO TICKETS! I AM GUARANTEED TO WIN!!

Okay, okay, you still want to know the mistake in that last strip, don't you? There's a watch on Goat's left arm in the third and fifth panels. But it's missing in the last panel.

Strip 2:

Panel 1: HEY, RAT, LOOK AT ME. I'M A BEEKEEPER! I EVEN GOT THE NET THING THAT THE BEES CAN'T GET THROUGH. / WHERE ARE THE BEES?

Panel 2: IN HERE. / OW!

Panel 3: YOU'D THINK THERE'D BE A BETTER WAY.

I've spent the last year or so pulling out ivy from around a new house we bought. And I've learned that ivy sometimes contains hornets' nests. When I say, "I've learned," I mean I've been stung twenty-two times.

Strip 3:

Panel 1: RAT'S THINKING ABOUT BUYING A PRIUS. / GOOD FOR YOU, RAT. BUYING A HYBRID IS A GREAT WAY TO SAVE GAS AND DO YOUR PART FOR THE ENVIRONMENT. / IT IS?

Panel 2: YEAH. WHY ELSE WOULD YOU BUY IT? / BECAUSE IT'S REAL QUIET, SO I THOUGHT IT'D BE PERFECT IF I EVER NEEDED TO RUN SOMEONE OVER FROM BEHIND.

Panel 3: AND HAVING LESS PEOPLE BENEFITS THE ENVIRONMENT! / THAT IS NOT HOW IT BENEFITS THE— / I'M DOING MY PART!!

After writing this strip, I learned that the quietness of these cars actually *is* a problem because pedestrians do not hear them coming. So some car manufacturers have begun manufacturing accessories that make the car louder.

For a while back in 2010, I was writing *Pearls* in a cafe in downtown Santa Rosa, California. Just outside the window of the cafe was this oddly shaped little dwarf tree. I thought it looked sort of funny, so I created this story line around it.

When I was a little kid, my best friend, Emilio, had a kumquat tree. And just over the back wall of his property was a big parking lot filled with people getting in and out of their cars. One might expect that two kids in that situation would spend every day of their summer throwing kumquats at those people. But not us. We were angels.

I'M DATING A GIRL WHO WANTS ME TO LEARN THE STUPID CHA CHA.
THAT'S A GREAT DANCE...I CAN TEACH YOU IF YOU WANT.
5/15
FINE. GIMME THE BASICS.
WELL, THE FIRST THING YOU GOTTA KNOW IS THAT IN THE CHA CHA, YOU LEAD WITH YOUR LEFT LEG AND ARM, WHICH WE'LL CALL YOUR CHA CHA LEG AND ARM.
FINE. WHAT ARE THE STEPS?
WELL, THE FIRST STEP IS TO STICK OUT YOUR CHA CHA LEG. THEN RAISE YOUR OPPOSITE ARM. THEN RAISE YOUR CHA CHA ARM.
DUDE, JUST SAY 'CHA' LEG OR SOMETHING. 'CHA CHA' IS SUCH A STUPID, FOO FOO WORD.
ALRIGHT, FINE. SO TRY IT. FIRST STICK OUT YOUR CHA LEG.
YEAH, YEAH, I KNOW. SECOND, RAISE MY OTHER ARM. THIRD, RAISE MY CHA LEG.
NO, NO...
THIRD TIME'S A CHA ARM.
DON'T MIND ME.
BEER
GASOLINE

Strip 1:

Panel 1: HEY, MISTER, YOU MIND MOVING OVER A LITTLE AND SHARING THE TREE? ME AND MY FRIENDS WANT TO BUILD A TREEHOUSE.

Panel 2: Share tree? Me deadly tree croc. Me no share tree wid leetle nobody peepsqueak.

Panel 3: You very rude.

When I was about seven years old, my dad built a clubhouse for me in the backyard. I put all my *Peanuts* comic strip books in it, and asked my cousin Jennifer to do the same. To this day, I still have her books.

Strip 2:

Panel 1: Hey, Bob, How Larry doing as deadly tree croc? / He say gud. He say when you deadly tree croc, you inteemidate whole world and no one mess wid you.

Panel 2: (silent)

Panel 3: Dis real low point for tree crocs, Bob. / Hey, Larry, stop playing hopscotch.

Prior to the nice wooden clubhouse my dad built, I had a cardboard clubhouse that I sent away for from some cereal company. Then it rained. And that was the end of that.

Strip 3:

Panel 1: Geet out of Keeds Club, Larry! Dis beeg shame to tree crocs. / Ohh, you gonna feel dumb for saying dat when me tell you whuh juss happen.

Panel 2: Whuh juss happen? / Me got elected vice president.

Panel 3: Geet out of tree, Larry. / One heartbeat from presidency, Bob.

Panel 1: HEY, RAT, WHAT'S THAT? / A SNUGGIE. IT'S A BLANKET WITH LITTLE SLEEVES SO YOU CAN STICK YOUR ARMS THROUGH IT.

Panel 2: WHY WOULD YOU NEED TO STICK YOUR ARMS THROUGH IT?

Panel 3: OOMF

Panel 4: YOU NEVER KNOW.

For the record, I have never owned a Snuggie.

Panel 1: HEY, MOM. WHY THE FAMILY MEETING? I WAS GONNA GO PLAY. / YOUR DAD HAS AN ANNOUNCEMENT, SON. AND JUDGING BY HIS SERIOUSNESS, I'D SAY IT'S PRETTY IMPORTANT.

Panel 2: SOME NEW HIGH-PAYING JOB? / EITHER THAT OR HE'S FINALLY TURNED INTO THE FIERCE HUNTER WE NEED HIM TO BE.

Panel 3: Me new Vice-President of Keeds Club Treehouse!!

Panel 4: GO PLAY, SON. / How come nobody bowing down?

Panel 1: HEY, GOAT, SORRY TO BOTHER YOU, BUT IF YOU KNOW THE GOOD FOLK WHO GIVE OUT THE NOBEL PRIZE FOR SCIENTIFIC BREAKTHROUGHS, COULD YOU PLEASE CALL THEM AND TELL THEM THERE'S NO NEED FOR DEBATE THIS YEAR. / WHY DO YOU SAY THAT?

Panel 2: IT'S GOING TO THE SNUGGIE GUY!!!

Panel 3: HAVE YOU CALLED THEM YET?

When I was in Stockholm, Sweden, a couple of years ago, I went to a cafe near where they award the Nobel Prizes every year. If you pick up any of the chairs in the cafe and look on the underside, you see the signatures of numerous Nobel Prize winners. I was tempted to draw Rat on one, but I chickened out.

Originally, I thought I would make this muse guy a regular character, but I haven't quite figured out how to use him.

Hey, I got away with saying "poopyhead." I just keep moving the comics page forward.

The prior day's strip had a "poopyhead." This day's strip has a guy who tries to kill his whole family. My, oh my, what will tomorrow bring?

43

Strip 1:

INSIDE THE KIDS CLUB TREEHOUSE

OKAY, FIRST ORDER OF BUSINESS IS WHAT WE CAN DO TO HELP SOMEONE IN OUR COMMUNITY. ....YES, TIMMY?

HOW 'BOUT THAT POOR ZEBRA WHO'S ALWAYS RUNNING FOR HIS LIFE? MAYBE WE COULD HELP HIM.

EES YOU ON DRUGS?!!

WILL THE VICE-PRESIDENT PLEASE TAKE HIS SEAT?

Okay...May me drop on Timmy's head?

Kids on drugs! Wow, no wonder people try to get *Pearls* booted from their paper.

Strip 2:

OKAY, YESTERDAY WE HAD SOME RUDENESS DURING OUR MEETING, SO I'M GONNA ASK EVERYONE TO PLEASE LIMIT THEIR COMMENTS TO CONSTRUCTIVE PROPOSALS...TIMMY, THE FLOOR IS YOURS.

OKAY, I PROPOSE THAT WE HELP THAT POOR ZEBRA WHO'S ALWAYS RUNNING FOR HIS LIFE BY BUILDING HIM A HUGE PROTECTIVE WALL.

Me propose we push Timmy out weendow.

HOW IS THAT CONSTRUCTIVE, LARRY?

Me want see if he can fly.

Strip 3:

HEY, RAT, I'D LIKE YOU TO MEET MY FRIEND, MEDUSA. SHE'S THAT REPULSIVE WOMAN FROM GREEK MYTHOLOGY.

I'VE HEARD OF MEDUSA. BUT SHE DOESN'T HAVE THOSE SNAKES IN HER HAIR...HOW CAN SHE BE REPULSIVE WITHOUT SNAKES?

SHE HAS LAWYERS.

Sue him. Bill him. Fleece him.

I THINK I'LL CHANGE SEATS.

Another crack at my former profession.

Mr. Stevie Sheep was tired of sheepdom.

So when his flock ate grass, Mr. Stevie ate berries.

And when his flock went, "Baaaaaaa," Mr. Stevie went, "Waaaaaaa."

BAAAA BAAAA BAAAA WAAAAA

And when his flock went into the meadow, Mr. Stevie went into the woods.

Where he could go "Waaaa" to his heart's content.

WAAAAA

Which, coincidentally, is the same sound made by an injured or otherwise vulnerable sheep.

WAAAAAAAAAAAAA

Which is how he met Mr. Wolf.

THIS IS YOUR INSPIRATIONAL 'BE YOURSELF' BOOK??

"SO, KIDS, BE YOURSELF, BUT MAKE SURE YOU DON'T SOUND LIKE A DYING SHEEP."

I WILL NEVER EVER BE MYSELF!

Strip 1 (5/30):

Goat: DO YOU REALIZE THAT WE'RE NOT GONNA LEARN THE IDENTITIES OF THESE NAVY SEAL GUYS THAT KILLED OSAMA BIN LADEN? THEY KEEP IT SECRET.

Rat: SO WE'LL NEVER KNOW WHO ACTUALLY PULLED THE TRIGGER?

Rat: THAT'S ONE MYSTERIOUS DUCK.

I drew this immediately after Osama bin Laden was killed and subbed it in to run sooner than it normally would. But in the interest of historical accuracy, I should add that I don't believe he was killed by a duck.

Strip 2 (5/31):

Customer: HI. GIMME A — OH, GREAT. AREN'T YOU THAT RUDE EMPLOYEE THAT WORKED HERE YEARS AGO?

Rat: YES, I'M BACK, BUT WITH A NEW GUARANTEE....I'M EITHER NICE TO YOU OR YOUR NEXT CUP'S FREE.

Customer: BUT WILL YOU BE RUDE THE NEXT TIME?

Rat: RUDER.

Customer: WHAT KIND OF DEAL IS THAT?

Rat: NOT A GOOD ONE, YOU OAFISH CHOWDERHEAD. OOPS....NEXT ONE'S ON ME.

Strip 3 (6/1):

Customer: HI, I'D LIKE A GRANDE, ONE PUMP, VANILLA, NONFAT, CARAMEL MACCHIATO.

Rat: AND I'D LIKE WORLD PEACE, BUT LO, IT'S NOT TO BE.

Customer: I TAKE IT I'M NOT GETTING MY ORDER.

Rat: SHHHH, I'M WISHING FOR UNICORNS TO DANCE UPON YOUR HEAD.

The only time I've ever really had a job where I had to interact with the public was when I was seventeen and worked at my uncle's restaurant in South Pasadena, California. It was called Gus's Barbeque. I made the salads.

46

Strip 1:

Panel 1: EXCUSE ME, RAT, BUT DO YOU KNOW WHY THERE'S A CUSTOMER SITTING IN OUR STORAGE ROOM? / OH, THAT GUY? YEAH, HE HAD A VERY COMPLICATED DRINK ORDER.

Panel 2: SO? / SO I GAVE HIM A TIME-OUT.

Panel 3: WE DO *NOT* DISCIPLINE OUR CUSTOMERS. / WHICH IS WHY THEY'RE OUT OF CONTROL. / MAY I COME OUT NOW?

This is probably the dream of many a person who works in the service industry.

Strip 2:

Panel 1: HI. GIMME AN ICED DOUBLE TALL NONFAT 180 VANILLA LATTE. / OKAY, BUT LET ME ASK YOU A QUESTION FIRST... ...YOU EVER HAD A HIGH-MAINTENANCE GIRLFRIEND?

Panel 2: YEAH, A WHILE BACK, I GUESS, BUT WE BROKE UP...WAIT... ...WHY YOU ASKING ME THIS? / BECAUSE YOU'RE A HIGH-MAINTENANCE CUSTOMER. AND I'M BREAKING UP WITH YOU.

Panel 3: GIMME MY G#T@G*# COFFEE. / CAN I HAVE A WORD WITH YOU, RAT? / FINE, BUT DON'T SERVE THE UGLY MAN. WE'VE BROKEN UP.

Strip 3:

Panel 1: HEY, NEIGHBOR BOB...HOW'S YOUR SON, WILLY? / OH, GREAT, PIG. HE JUST TURNED TWELVE AND STARTED SEVENTH GRADE.

Panel 2: TWELVE, HUH? WHAT A WONDERFUL AGE! YOU'VE GOT FRIENDS, SOCCER, VIDEO GAMES, SUMMER CAMP...IS HE ENJOYING IT ALL? / OH, YEAH...AND ALL I'VE ASKED HIM TO DO IS TO MAKE SURE HE MAINTAINS A PERFECT 4.0.

Panel 3: YAAAAY, CHILDHOOD. / OH... ...HI, WILLY. / *SHHHH.* HE WON'T GET INTO YALE.

Sadly, I think I was a lot like Willy when I was a kid; I was always worried about getting a high GPA so I could get into a good college. Had I known that one day I would be a slacker cartoonist, I would have spent a lot less time worrying.

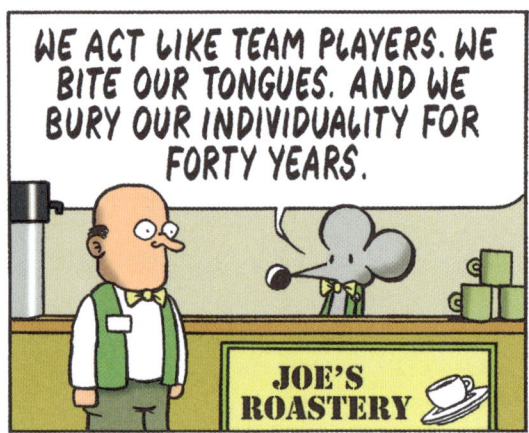

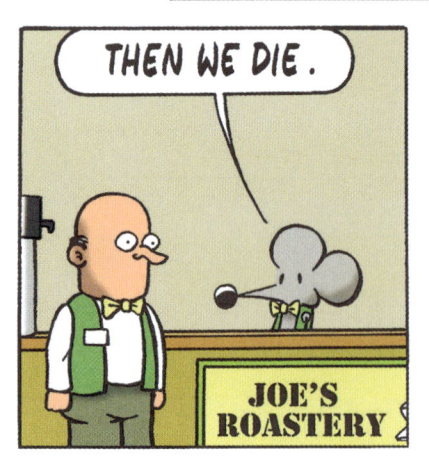

Panel 1: LISTEN, RAT... YOU NEED TO START THINKING ABOUT YOUR CAREER PATH WITH JOE'S ROASTERY... IT OFFERS GREAT BENEFITS. HERE'S HOW I SEE A CORPORATE CAREER.

Panel 2: I ACT LIKE SOMEONE I'M NOT TO GET AHEAD.... YOU ACT LIKE SOMEONE YOU'RE NOT TO GET AHEAD.

Panel 3: WE BOTH PRETEND LIKE WE CARE ABOUT EACH OTHER'S FAMILIES. WE SOMETIMES GRAB A BEER.

Panel 4: WE GO TO THE PARTIES WE HAVE TO. WE SMILE WHEN WE NEED TO. WE PRAISE WHO WE MUST.

Panel 5: WE ACT LIKE TEAM PLAYERS. WE BITE OUR TONGUES. AND WE BURY OUR INDIVIDUALITY FOR FORTY YEARS.

Panel 6: THEN WE DIE.

Panel 7: IF YOU'LL EXCUSE ME, I'M GONNA SELL ALL MY POSSESSIONS AND BACKPACK THROUGH NEPAL.

Panel 8: I'M GOOD FOR MORALE.

I think I was trying to describe the life that remained for me had I remained a lawyer. Phew. That was a close call.

Panel 1 (Strip 1):
- "LISTEN, LARRY..."
- "'...Meester Vice Pressydent Larry.'"
- "OH, GIVE IT UP, LARRY. I'M NOT GONNA CALL YOU 'MR. VICE PRESIDENT.' YOU'RE THE VICE-PRESIDENT OF A LITTLE KIDS' TREEHOUSE."
- "For now."
- "FOR NOW?"
- "Me gonna stage coup."
- "GET OUT OF THE BED, LARRY."
- "'Meester Vice Pressydent Larry.'"

That would be a very uncomfortable hat to sleep in.

Strip 2: LARRY PLANS HIS TREEHOUSE COUP
- "Okay, guys, Meester Vice Pressydent Larry ask you here becuss me need you help een very eemportant meeshun."
- "Whuh dat?"
- "Me revolting."
- "No, you not, Larry. You juss leetle bit ugly."
- "Mebbe me no need you help, Bob."
- "Mebbe juss geet new face, you be okay, Larry."

Strip 3:
- "HEY, PIG. WHERE YOU BEEN?"
- "GETTING MY TOMBSTONE MADE... I ALWAYS LIKE TO PLAN AHEAD... I TOLD THE GUY TO GIVE ME A REAL NICE EPITHET."
- "'EPITAPH.'....'EPITHET' IS AN INSULT."
- "NUTS."
- (Tombstone: PIG A #$&%$&# IDIOT)

One time I was watching the closed caption version of CNN (where you can read what is being said at the bottom of the screen), and the person doing the closed captioning used the word "epithet" when what was said was "epitaph." I thought it was really funny. And thus, I wrote this strip.

49

LARRY PLANS HIS TREEHOUSE COUP

Hey, leetle duck... Me know you like fat peegy guy, but me want buy you services for eemportant meeshun.

HMMM.. LET ME THINK ABOUT THAT.

RAT A TAT A TAT A TAT A TAT

Is you done tinking?

Those guns are very hard for me to draw, so there might have been some cutting and pasting going on between the third and fourth panels. Hey, I'm not gonna draw the darn thing *twice*.

HEY, CARTOON BOY, THERE'S A WORD FOR WHEN A PERSON HAS TO GO 'NUMBER TWO' THAT BEGINS WITH A 'P.' CAN WE USE IT ON THE COMICS PAGE OR WILL 'THE MAN' STOP US?

WE CAN'T USE IT.

GEE, THAT'S STRICT. AM I ALLOWED TO SHOW YOU THE DIFFERENT PARTS OF THIS MODEL SHIP I JUST BUILT OR IS THAT BANNED TOO?

I DON'T KNOW WHAT THAT HAS TO DO WITH YOUR LAST QUESTION, BUT YEAH, OF COURSE YOU CAN.

GOOD. THAT'S THE POOP DECK.

ENOUGH.

A WHOLE DECK FOR *THAT*?!

Just a couple weeks after saying "poopy," I got away with saying "poop." Take a couple moments to applaud.

PIG, TAKE A MEMO... I HAVE A FINAL WISH THAT I'D LIKE YOU, MY FRIENDS, TO TAKE NOTE OF AND FULFILL SHOULD I DIE AN UNTIMELY DEATH.

SURE, RAT, WHAT IS IT?

I'D LIKE YOU, TOO, TO STOP LIVING.

YOU MIGHT BE A LITTLE VAIN.

OH, AND MAKE THE WORLD STOP. IT SHOULDN'T GO ON WITHOUT ME.

'STOP... WHOLE... WORLD...'

It depresses me to no end to think that the world can go on without me. That just seems wrong.

I'm a fan of the radio show *This American Life*. But surprisingly, after this strip was published, I did not hear from anyone on the show. Perhaps my beatdown of the host offended someone.

LARRY'S TREEHOUSE COUP

EXCUSE ME, MR. PRESIDENT, BUT I'D LIKE TO MAKE A MOTION THAT WE IMPEACH VICE PRESIDENT LARRY. I SUSPECT HIM OF DISLOYALTY.

WHY DO YOU SAY THAT?

Me juss doing leetle pruning.

LARRY, THE KIDS CLUB TREEHOUSE HAS VOTED TO KICK YOU OUT OF THE GROUP... PLEASE TURN IN YOUR HAT.

HA! Me keeck YOU out! Me geet frends help me een beeg coup!

LARRY, YOU'RE MISTAKENLY PRONOUNCING THE 'P' IN 'COUP.' THE 'P' IS SILENT. SO WHEN YOU SAY IT YOUR WAY, IT HAS A WHOLE DIFFERENT MEANING.

HA! Whuh da heck you know, Meester Inteelecktual!

How dis help Larry?

My daughter used to raise chickens at her grandmother's house. But then the chickens died. Given that they did nothing but peck me, I do not miss them.

HEY, DAD... WHAT HAPPENED TO YOUR VICE PRESIDENT'S HAT?

Me got keecked out. Me no want talk about it.

GEE, DAD, I'M SORRY. WHAT ARE YOU GONNA DO NOW?

Me form own club, Club One Guy. Is guy who juss sit alone in box.

CAN IT BE 'CLUB TWO GUY'?

Okay. But me gonna have to change stationery.

Awwww. That's kinda touching. Especially after my callous comment about the chickens.

Panel 1:
- WHEN DO YOU THINK YOU BECOME MIDDLE-AGED?
- WHEN ON A SUMMER VACATION, YOU TUCK A COLLARED SHIRT INTO KHAKI SHORTS HELD UP BY A BELT.

Panel 2:
- OKAY, SWEETIE, 'FROMMER'S' SAYS THE VIEW HERE IS DELIGHTFUL.

Panel 3:
- IT SCARES ME WHEN YOU'RE ACCURATE.
- WELL, SIR, THAT'S A HAT YOU WOULDN'T HAVE WORN WHEN YOU STILL CARED.

Okay, all kidding aside, this is totally true. Once you wear the khaki shorts and belt on vacation, you can kiss your youth good-bye.

Panel 4:
- HEY, NEIGHBOR BOB. HOW GOES IT?
- GREAT, PIG... JUST GOT BACK FROM VACATION. I WAS ABLE TO TAKE A TON OF GOOD PHOTOS. HERE, LET ME SHOW YOU.

Panel 5:
- CRACK! HOP

Panel 6:
- IT'S THE BEST WAY TO HANDLE THAT.

And after you wear those khaki shorts on vacation, we don't want to see your photos either.

Panel 7:
- WHERE WERE YOU THIS MORNING?
- AT HOME. I'VE BEEN SPENDING EVERY SINGLE MORNING LISTENING TO THIS REALLY CALMING RADIO STATION.

Panel 8:
- OH, YEAH? DO YOU KNOW THE FREQUENCY?
- I JUST TOLD YOU.

Panel 9:
- TOLD ME WHAT?
- I LISTEN TO IT EVERY SINGLE MORNING.

Panel 10:
- DO YOU KNOW THE FREQUENCY WITH WHICH I WANT TO PUNCH YOU ANGRILY IN THE HEAD?
- OOOOH. HAVE I GOT THE RADIO STATION FOR YOU.

I am proud to say I have never gone to a 3D movie. But then again, I rarely leave home.

Panel 1:
- DID YOU KNOW THAT SOME BOTTLED WATER IS JUST CITY WATER RE-PACKAGED?

Panel 2:
- ARE YOU KIDDING ME? YOU MEAN SOME GUYS JUST BOTTLE THE STUFF I ALREADY GET OUT OF MY OWN TAP AND SELL IT BACK TO ME FOR A HIGHER PRICE?
- YUP. HOW DOES THAT MAKE YOU FEEL?

Panel 3:
- FILL, YOU FAT PIG, FILL!!!
- RAT WATER, INC.

What Goat says in the first panel is actually true. It has really stopped me from buying certain kinds of bottled water.

Panel 4:
- HI, GOAT, CAN I INTEREST YOU IN OUR NEW PRODUCT? IT'S BOTTLED WATER. SEE, IT'S GOT A BEAUTIFUL MOUNTAIN SPRING ON THE LABEL. I EVEN GAVE IT A FANCY FRENCH-SOUNDING NAME: 'Le LAVABO.'

Panel 5:
- 'LeLAVABO' MEANS 'BATHROOM SINK.'

Panel 6:
- NUTS. I'VE GIVEN AWAY MY SECRET SOURCE.
- GO AWAY.
- IF IT MAKES YOU FEEL BETTER, SOME OF IT COMES FROM OUR TUB.

Looks to me like a lazy cartoonist drew that bottle just one time and then cut and pasted it dozens of times. The nerve.

Panel 7:
- DID YOU BY CHANCE TELL PIG ABOUT AN UPCOMING MOVIE?
- YEAH. THE NEW COEN BROTHERS FILM...IT LOOKS GREAT, SO I TOLD HIM TO GO CHECK OUT THE TRAILER....WHY?

Panel 8:
(Pig standing next to a trailer)

Panel 9:
- BECAUSE YOU NEED TO BE MORE SPECIFIC.
- ABOUT WHAT?
- THE FACT THAT IT'S BO-O-O-ORING

55

I can't tell you how excited some readers get when Rat gets smacked. I guess they like to see him get his comeuppance. (And did I really just use the word "comeuppance"? Apparently, I'm eighty-five years old.)

I cannot build the simplest thing. If there is any assembly required at all, I either start crying or give it to my wife.

Clive is a real person. He is the owner of the cafe where I often write the strip. He now has a print of this strip on the wall of the cafe.

"Ohhh... Me could catch heem."
"Yeah. Me could catch too."

"Me could tear off dat guy head."
"Yeah. Me would reep to shred."

"Ooooh, me could so keel dat one!"
"Yeah, me would eet in seconds!"

"DAD, I KNOW YOU AND BOB ARE TOUGH, BUT YOU MAKE IT REALLY HARD TO WATCH 'THE MUPPETS.'"

"Told you dat not nature documentary."

Muppets would probably taste great.

Speaking of long appendages, Rat's snout is waaaay too long in that last panel.

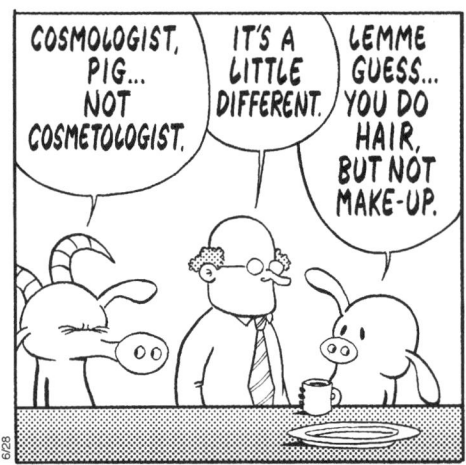

This was a lesson I learned in dealing with my own wife. Which I can say because she doesn't read these treasuries. BWAHAHAHAAA.

I still hate emoticons. Especially the winking variety.

I must have changed Pig's line in the last panel at least six different times because I just couldn't decide which was the best punch line. I'm still not sure I got it right. It's a little too wordy.

I don't think I could have gotten away with this strip in my first couple years of syndication. But now that I've done the strip for twelve years, I think that my syndicate gives me *slightly* more leeway.

Speaking of leeway, I always try to use the same number of swear squiggles as there are letters in the swear word (e.g., if the word I'm trying to convey is "damn," there would be four swear squiggles). But when the character says "(Blank) you" to someone, and that word is four letters long, it pretty clearly telegraphs the "F" word. And that I *don't* have leeway to convey. So here I used five swear squiggles to telegraph the word "screw." Thus, the fish is saying, "Screw you, pal." A much less problematic phrase.

Panel 1:
- Rat: WHAT THE.... ...LOOK! IT'S AN ALIEN SPACESHIP.
- Pig: OH MY GOODNESS! ALIENS! WHAT WILL THEY LOOK LIKE? HOW WILL WE GET ALONG?

Panel 3:
- I SENSE A CLASH OF CIVILIZATIONS.

The way you know that's an alien spaceship is that in the first panel, Rat says, "Look! It's an alien spaceship."

Strip 2, Panel 1: RAT AND PIG MEET AN ALIEN RACE.
- WE HAVE ASKED FOR THIS SUMMIT TO DISCUSS OUR RESPECTIVE GOALS. OURS IS TO PROMOTE INTERPLANETARY PEACE THROUGH THE EXCHANGE OF TECHNOLOGY AND CULTURE.

Panel 2: MINE IS TO DRINK YOUR HEAD.

Panel 3: IF IT'S ANY CONSOLATION, I'LL RECYCLE THE CAN.

And the way you know that's beer is that it says "BEER" on it. Drawing is easy if you tell people in words exactly what they're looking at.

Strip 3, Panel 1: RAT AND PIG MEET AN ALIEN RACE
- THANK YOU, PIG FRIEND, FOR PARTICIPATING IN OUR INTERPLANETARY SUMMIT. MAY THE PEACE WE FORGED BE THE FIRST STEP IN A LONG AND PRODUCTIVE ALLIANCE.
- YES! A TOAST TO US!

Panel 2: GLUG GLUG GLUG GLUG

Panel 3: NEXT TIME, LET'S SKIP THE TOAST.

Oddly, the tabs on the beer cans are all already opened, implying that someone else has been swigging beer out of these poor guys' heads.

Zeeba neighba...Come heres.
WHAT DO YOU WANT?
Time geev up. Crocs find you mail slot.
SO?
So me tell Bob buy essplosives, shove een heres.
Me thought you say 'Shove een ears.'
KABOOM
We having techneecal deeficulties.

Panel 1:
HEY, GOAT, WANT TO COME WITH ME AND GUARD DUCK ON OUR JOURNEY THROUGH SPACE?

Panel 2:
HAHAHA...WELL, GOSH, PIG, I'D LOVE TO PLAY WITH YOU TWO IN THAT BIG CARDBOARD BOX, BUT I'VE GOTTA RUN TO THE BANK...SO YOU GUYS HAVE FUN.

Panel 3:
HE LOOKED SURPRISED WHEN THE ROCKET BOOSTERS KICKED IN.

I'm sure I was inspired by *Calvin and Hobbes* here. What a ridiculously great strip that was.

Panel 4:
ALRIGHT, SUPPLY OFFICER DUCK, NOW THAT WE'RE IN SPACE, WE SHOULD GO THROUGH OUR 'THREE ESSENTIAL ITEMS CHECKLIST.'...LET'S SEE.....PEANUT BUTTER? CHECK. ROOT BEER? CHECK. OXYGEN SUPPLY?

Panel 6:
IT'S VERY TASTY PEANUT BUTTER.

Panel 7:
PIG'S GREAT SPACE JOURNEY
IT SAYS HERE THAT IN 2006, SCIENTISTS DECLARED THAT PLUTO WAS NO LONGER TO BE CONSIDERED ONE OF OUR NINE PLANETS. INSTEAD, ITS CLASSIFICATION WAS LOWERED TO THAT OF A 'DWARF' PLANET.

Panel 9:
HE TOOK IT HARD.
WAS 'DRUNKY' ONE OF THE SEVEN DWARFS?

"Drunky" was not one of the original seven dwarves. But "Deafy" almost was. I swear. Look it up.

Strip 1:

Rat: HEY, MORON...LAST WEEK YOU DROPPED A STORYLINE WITH ANGRY BEER CAN ALIENS. THIS WEEK YOU LEFT PIG IN SPACE WITH NO OXYGEN. EVER PLAN ON ACTUALLY *FINISHING* A @#$&#@ STORYLINE?

Alien 1: THERE'S THE ENEMY! THROW SOMETHING HEAVY AT THEM!
Alien 2: I'LL HIT 'EM WITH THESE OXYGEN TANKS!
Pig: WE'RE SAVED!

Rat: TELL ME THEY DON'T PAY YOU FOR THIS.

I really couldn't come up with an ending for either series. So I made a joke out of ending both of them badly.

Strip 2:

Goat: WHERE'S RAT TODAY?
Pig: HE GOT A JOB AS A TV NEWS ANCHOR.
Goat: SINCE WHEN DID HE TAKE AN INTEREST IN TV NEWS?
Pig: SINCE HE LEARNED THAT THEY LIKE TO DO STORIES BASED ON FEAR.

Rat: TONIGHT AT SIX... HOW FAT DWARVES ARE PLANNING TO EAT YOU.
(DWARF THREAT)

Two dwarf strips in three days. Not bad.

Strip 3:

IN THE CHANNEL 7 NEWSROOM
Anchor: I DON'T GET IT, RAT. OUR RATINGS ARE UP TEN PERCENT SINCE YOU CAME HERE. HOW DO YOU DO IT?
Rat: FEAR. FEAR. FEAR. FEAR. FEAR.

Anchor: FEAR, HUH? BUT HOW?
Rat: I'LL SHOW YOU. NAME SOMETHING WE ALL HAVE IN OUR HOUSE AND SOMETHING WE ALL DO.

Anchor: UH.....MAYONNAISE... SLEEP.
Rat: TONIGHT AT SIX... HOW YOUR MAYONNAISE JAR MAY BE TRYING TO SUFFOCATE YOU IN YOUR SLEEP.

Anchor: WOW.
Rat: AT ELEVEN... HOW YOU CAN PROTECT YOURSELF FROM YOUR HOMICIDAL MAYONNAISE.

This really is me at parties. While I don't actually sit in a closet, I do try to find where they keep their books. Then I just sit there and read.

| "AREN'T YOU TIRED OF A GOVERNMENT THAT IS OWNED AND CONTROLLED BY BIG INTERESTS AND A SUPREME COURT THAT SAYS IT'S OKAY?" "I SURE AM. WE REALLY NEED TO ORGANIZE AND—" | "OVERTHROW IT!!!" | "I WAS GONNA SUGGEST TOWN HALL MEETINGS." "GOOD IDEA. WE CAN HAND OUT THE PITCHFORKS THERE." |

| "WHAT ARE YOU DOING, RAT?" "I'M ADVOCATING THE OVERTHROW OF THE GOVERNMENT." | "THEY'LL TOSS YOU IN THE POKEY!" "THEY CAN'T. I'M JUST A FICTIONAL CARTOON CHARACTER. THEY HAVE ABSOLUTELY NO RECOURSE WHATSOEVER." | [FBI agents at S. Pastis's desk] |

I do sometimes wonder what would happen if I openly advocated revolution in the comic strip. Could I really be arrested? Maybe I can convince *Family Circus* creator Jeff Keane to try it first.

| "MOM, THIS IS STEPHAN...LISTEN, I GOT THROWN IN JAIL BECAUSE ONE OF MY CHARACTERS ADVOCATED REVOLUTION. NOW LISTEN...YOU'RE MY ONE CALL SO I NEED YOU TO—" | "SORRY, SON...BUSY PLAYING 'ANGRY BIRDS' ON MY iPAD." | "I NEVER WAS HER FAVORITE KID." |

I think I've said this before, but truly, my mother does not like the way she's portrayed in the strip. Mostly because people come up to her and say, "Patti, I didn't know you smoked." Which she doesn't. Maybe I should push the envelope even more and give her character a serious drug addiction.

If you look at the weather map in the fourth panel very closely, you'll see that there is rain forecast for somewhere over Idaho. That's the kind of attention to detail you pay me for.

Sadly, *Jiffy and Spiffy* would be more entertaining than most newspaper comic strips.

Little did you know that Pluto was actually this small. That's why it's no longer a planet.

68

If you Google my name and the word "Facebook," you need only type the "F" in "Facebook" and then Google will immediately prompt you with the rest of the word. Meaning that a lot of people Google "Stephan Pastis Facebook." Interestingly, though, if you Google my name and then just type the letter "j," Google will prompt you with the word "jail." Meaning that a lot of people Google "Stephan Pastis jail." That tells me that a fair number of people were curious as to whether or not I had truly been sent to jail.

My poor Mom.

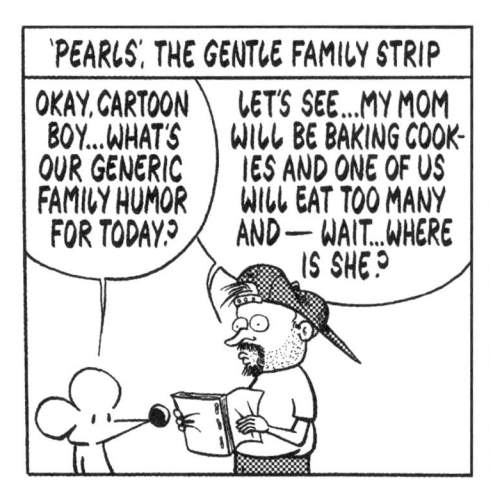

My mother would like you to know she has never fired a gun in her life. Nor does she swear. She has, however, had a beer.

After I drew this strip, I e-mailed it to the *Dennis the Menace* creators and asked if they wanted to make fun of *Pearls* in their strip on the same day mine would appear in newspapers. They were great sports about it and actually drew me (Stephan) in that same day's *Dennis the Menace*. In their strip, Dennis is making fun of me for not having a real job. The original now hangs in my studio.

While I told the *Dennis* creators about the prior *Dennis* strip, I did not tell them about this one. I'm not quite sure why. Maybe I thought I'd be pushing my luck.

71

WHAT ARE YOU EATING, GOAT?
OATMEAL FROM THIS NEW COMPANY... IT'S MADE FROM ONLY THE FRESHEST OATS.
WHY IS THAT IMPORTANT?
BECAUSE WHEN OTHER COMPANIES USE OLD OATS, THE TASTE IS NOT AS GOOD.
THEN WHY DO OTHERS USE OLD OATS?
I DON'T KNOW, BUT MAYBE THAT WOULD BE A GOOD SLOGAN FOR THIS NEW COMPANY. THEY'RE HOLDING A CONTEST.
YEAH. IT COULD JUST BE 'WHY OLD OATS?'
YEAH. ALL YOU HAVE TO DO IS PUT IT ON AN ARTICLE OF CLOTHING AND TAKE A PHOTO OF IT.
I'LL GET MY NEEDLE AND THREAD AND START RIGHT NOW!
KNOCK
KNOCK
KNOCK
OH. HEY, PIGITA.
HELLO, PIG. I CAME BY TO SEE IF YOU'D LIKE TO GO TO DINNER WITH ME.
CAN'T. I'M ABOUT TO SEW MY 'WHY OLD OATS.'
MY GIRLFRIEND IS NOT VERY SUPPORTIVE.

THE DEPARTMENT OF JUSTICE

Per the plea agreement with Stephan Pastis, last week's strips were to be family-friendly.

Instead, they depicted an inebriated mother, a sociopathic frog, and Dennis the Menace as an arsonist.

As these offensive strips contained everything but a gun-toting, Communist monkey, the strip has been handed over to a guest artist, and Stephan's bail has been set at one million dollars.

BANG BANG

Make that two million.

I can say with certainty that this is the first gun-toting, Communist monkey to appear on the American comics page.

STEPHAN IN FEDERAL PRISON

HEY, PRISON BOY... THE COURT'S APPOINTED YOU A LAWYER FOR YOUR TRIAL.

I THOUGHT I WAS GONNA HAVE TO REPRESENT MYSELF.

I'LL REPRESENT MYSELF.

HELLO... WE'D LIKE TO PLEAD MORONITY.

STEPHAN'S FEDERAL TRIAL

I CANNOT BELIEVE YOU'RE MY LAWYER.

CHILL, TOON BOY. YOU'RE IN THE HANDS OF A PRO.

AND HOW DOES THE DEFENDANT PLEAD?

GUILTY, YOUR HONOR. AND WE'D LIKE TO ASK FOR THE DEATH PENALTY.

THE WHAT?!!

YEAH. I PROBABLY SHOULD HAVE MENTIONED THAT.

I made a rather big mistake in this strip. See if you can find it yourself. I'll reveal the answer in the next comment.

ANSWER TO QUESTION ABOUT LAST STRIP: In the first and third panels, I am sitting on Rat's right. In the second panel, I am seated on his left. Bonus *Pearls* points if you caught that.

I always feel odd drawing myself without my trademark backwards cap. It makes my character look almost unrecognizable.

Sometimes at book signings, people will ask me to draw an RPG (the item held here by Guard Duck). But there's just no way. While I can draw the Guard Duck in under thirty seconds, the RPG takes me around fifteen minutes, and even then, I have to be looking at a photo of one.

CABLE'S OUT AGAIN.
THAT DOES IT. I'M GONNA CALL THOSE CABLE IDIOTS AND RIP INTO 'EM.
8-7
BOMBAST CABLE. HOW CAN WE HELP YOU?
YEAH. I—
IS THIS A LIVE PERSON IN THIS COUNTRY?
YEP.
NO 'PRESS 1 FOR THIS,' 'PRESS 2 FOR THAT' AND THEN BEING ON HOLD FOR AN HOUR?
NOPE.
YEAH, WELL, I BET YOU STILL CAN'T GET OUT HERE 'TIL NEXT WEEK.
NOT TRUE. WE CAN BE THERE TODAY.
REALLY?
REALLY.
WELL, I BET THE BEST YOU CAN DO IS GIVE ME A FOUR-HOUR WINDOW IN WHICH YOU *MIGHT* BE HERE.
NOPE. WE'LL BE THERE AT 3:00 P.M. ON THE DOT.
AN EXACT TIME?
YEP.
IS THIS A DREAM?
YEP.

Panel 1:
- Judge: MR. PASTIS, TELL THE JURY IN YOUR OWN WORDS WHY THEY SHOULD REFRAIN FROM THROWING YOU IN THE CLINK.
- Pastis: WELL... I DO THESE ELABORATE PUN STRIPS, AND I THINK THEY'RE SORT OF POPULAR, AND IF I WAS PUT AWAY FOR LIFE, THERE'D NEVER BE ANOTHER ONE.

Panel 2:
- Jury: YAAAAAAAAAAAAY

Panel 3:
- Judge: YAAAAY. YAAAAY. I GIVE UP.

That looks like an all-white jury. So I apparently live in a very racist town.

Panel 4:
- Lawyer: OKAY, JUST TO PREPARE YOU, THE GOVERNMENT'S NEXT WITNESS IS REALLY GONNA TRY TO TEAR YOU APART. HE'S GONNA TELL THE JURY YOU'RE A LIAR AND A FRAUD AND THAT YOU SHOULD SPEND THE REST OF YOUR LIFE BEHIND BARS.

Panel 5:
- Pastis: OH, GREAT... WHO IS IT?

Panel 6:
- Judge: DO YOU PROMISE TO TELL THE WHOLE TRUTH AND NOTHING BUT THE TRUTH?
- Rat: OH, BOY, DO I!

Panel 7:
- Pastis: STEPHAN'S FEDERAL TRIAL. RAT! WHERE ARE YOU? TODAY'S THE DAY FOR CLOSING ARGUMENTS AND YOU'RE MY LAWYER!

Panel 8:
- Rat: SORRY. CAN'T MAKE IT. I'M UNDER A BIT OF A TIME CONSTRAINT.
- Pastis: TIME CONSTRAINT? WHAT TIME CONSTRAINT?

Panel 9:
- Rat: TO FINISH THE BEER IN MY COOLER BEFORE IT GETS WARM.

Panel 10:
- Pastis: I'M FACING LIFE IN PRISON.
- Rat: AND I'M FACING WARM BEER. PLEASE, MAN, PRIORITIZE.

I went to England in 2012 and the beer they served in bars was warm. That's probably why they almost lost World War II.

In the actual *Pluggers* comic strip, the creators often thank the person who sent in the idea. Thus, the "thanks" in the last panel. But in my last panel, I've chosen to thank my best friend, Emilio, who had nothing to do with this strip, but whose full name and hometown I wanted to display in the hopes that people would look up his phone number and annoy him to no end. Sadly, he has an unlisted number.

A tribute to my cartooning hero, Charles "Sparky" Schulz.

The sheep were angry.

Angry about their old barn. Angry about their bad food. Angry about getting sheared.

"Let's band together and tell Farmer Bob how we feel," said Stevie Sheep. "For together we are strong."

So all the sheep marched together to see Farmer Bob.

"What the #%&# do you want?" asked Farmer Bob, holding out the biggest pair of shears any of the sheep had ever seen.

"Me and my united sheep brothers wish to present you with some demands," said Stevie Sheep.

"What sheep brothers?" asked Farmer Bob.

Stevie Sheep was sheared like he was never sheared before.

THIS IS YOUR 'GUIDE TO BEING A TEAM PLAYER'?!

"SO REMEMBER, KIDS, NEVER BE THE ONE TO SPEAK UP."

I AM NOT SAYING A WORD.

The most accurate depiction of human nature ever to appear in *Pearls*.

Panel row 1:

— WHUH YOU TINK YOU DOEENG?!
— BUILDING THE WALL HIGHER. I SHOULD HAVE DONE THIS YEARS AGO.
— But you hurteeng our relashunsheep.
— RELATIONSHIP? YOU JUST KEPT TRYING TO KILL ME.
— Try to focus on da gud times.

At first, I thought this wall was a good idea for a series. Then I had to draw the thing. And boy, did I start regretting the wall series.

Panel row 2:

— DID YOU HEAR THOSE TREEHOUSE KIDS BUILT A BIG WALL FOR ZEBRA?
— YEAH. I MET THEM. THEY'RE SUCH GOOD, DEPENDABLE KIDS. ZEBRA AND I REALLY SWEAR BY THEM.
— THAT'S WRONG.
— WHAT'S WRONG?
— TEACHING PROFANITY TO LITTLE KIDS.
— NEVER MIND.
— SORRY. I'VE GOT A FOUL-MOUTHED FRIEND.

Panel row 3:

— WHAT ARE THE CROCS DOING?
— THEY WANT ME TO GET RID OF MY WALL, SO THEY HIRED A POLITICAL CONSULTANT TO HELP THEM FIGURE OUT THE MOST EFFECTIVE APPROACH.
— MEESTER ZEEBACHEV... TEAR DOWN DIS WALL!!
— DID RONALD REAGAN CONCLUDE BY THROWING BEER CANS?
— HEY! RECYCLE THOSE!

This is a reference to Ronald Reagan's famous line to the Soviet leader Mikhail Gorbachev, "Mr. Gorbachev, tear down this wall." I believe this is the second time the quote has appeared in *Pearls*.

That is not a bad crib. My artistry grows with each passing year.

Every time I ever lost something, my mom would tell me to retrace my steps. That got very annoying. What got even more annoying was that it worked.

80

I took every one of these warnings from an actual toaster manual.

Panel 1: "HEY... WHAT THE G#☆#'S THIS?" "A WALL TO KEEP THE CROCS OUT... AND THAT'S A SECURITY GATE I HAD THIS MAN INSTALL. IT CAN ONLY BE OPENED BY ENTERING THE TOP-SECRET SECURITY PASSWORD."

Panel 2: "SO IS IT '1-2-3-4,' 'PASSWORD,' OR YOUR BIRTHDAY?"

Panel 3: "WE SHOULD CHANGE THE TOP-SECRET SECURITY CODE."

I looked up "most common security passwords" on the internet, and the ones Rat lists were the most common. And right now, you're changing your security passwords.

Panel 4: "Hey zeebs...Crocs make you ice cream cake to say we truly sorry for past meestakes..... Oh, no. Ice cream melting and me no can fit through bars."

Panel 5: "Oh, well. Guess you has to open gate."

Panel 6: "He no leesten gud."

Panel 7: "Hey, Melvin. Me do grocery shopping dis week for our Zeeba Zeeba Eata fraternity. And you no do no chore at all." "So?"

Panel 8: "So strap bomb to youself and blow up wall."

Panel 9: "Me feel like you got better part of deal."

Ugh! More of this darn wall. My poor drawing hand.

Panel 1:
- "Hey, Bob. When bomb blow up?"
- "Toomorrow at noon, Melvin."

Panel 2:
- "Well, better be quick 'cause me has busy afternoon."

Panel 3:
- "Melvin seem unclear on concept."

Some people get upset when I depict a character with a bomb strapped to his chest, because they say it too closely mimics violence that happens in real life. I ignore those people.

Panel 4:
- "Leesten, Larry...Me no happy you make me volunteer blow self up, and me want you know me is do someting geet even."
- "Whuh you do?"

Panel 5:
- "Me unfriend you on Facebook."

Panel 6:
- "Dat low blow, Melvin."

Panel 7:
- "HEY, GOAT! GOAT! I FINALLY GOT A DATE!"
- "GOOD FOR YOU, PIG! HOW'D THAT COME ABOUT? THE PERSONALS? MATCH.COM?"

Panel 8:
- "THE GROCERY STORE."

Panel 9:
- "NEVER MIND."
- "DOES MATCH.COM SELL FRUIT?"

That's supposed to be a date on the table in front of Pig. It is not, as you may have been wondering, a hamster.

83

Okay. It's bad form to call your own strips funny. But this strip really makes me laugh.

THE PLOT TO DESTROY ZEBRA'S WALL

Hey, Larry... When Melvin's bomb s'pose go off?

Any meenute now. Dat why we wait here een safety of fraternity house.

Sorry, but me got take queek potty break.

Dis bad time read on john.

Hey, Melvin... Me and Bob no want hurry you potty break, but you has beeg bomb strapped to you.

Hey, when you rush Melvin potty break, Melvin internal organs no work right. Beeside, me no done reading newspaper.

Newspaper? How much you has left?

Juss New York Times crossword puzzle...Sunday eedition.

Dis not gud sign, Bob.

Whoa...Dis one harder den Monday's.

I am proud to say that in 2012, a Sunday crossword puzzle in the *New York Times* had the clue, "Comic strip with Rat and Pig." I knew the answer.

LOOK AT THIS...I'M TRYING TO TAPE DOWN THE LOOSE BACK OF THE T.V. REMOTE, BUT THE END OF MY SCOTCH TAPE ROLL GOT STUCK SOMEWHERE BACK ON THE ROLL. NOW IT'S IMPOSSIBLE TO FIND THE END, MUCH LESS PEEL IT OFF.

SO?

SO NOW MY WHOLE WEEK IS RUINED.

HE'S A TAD TIGHTLY WOUND.

WELL, TIME TO DESTROY THE WHOLE T.V.

85

This became a popular image of Pig. Some people even used it as their profile picture on Facebook.

"Crap" is an iffy word on the comics page. Sometimes you can get away with it and sometimes you can't. So I used its less offensive cousin, "crappo."

86

Oh, thank goodness. The wall is almost gone.

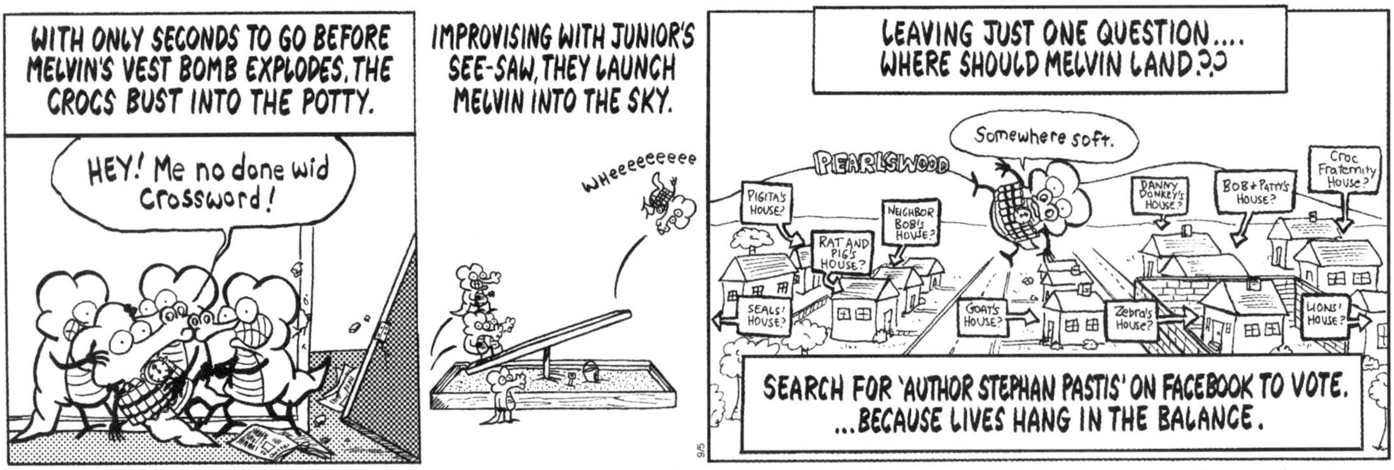
WITH ONLY SECONDS TO GO BEFORE MELVIN'S VEST BOMB EXPLODES, THE CROCS BUST INTO THE POTTY.
HEY! Me no done wid crossword!
IMPROVISING WITH JUNIOR'S SEE-SAW, THEY LAUNCH MELVIN INTO THE SKY.
WHeeeeeeeee
LEAVING JUST ONE QUESTION.... WHERE SHOULD MELVIN LAND???
Somewhere soft.
PEARLSWOOD
PIGITA'S HOUSE?
RAT AND PIG'S HOUSE?
NEIGHBOR BOB'S HOUSE?
DANNY DONKEY'S HOUSE?
BOB + PATTY'S HOUSE?
Croc Fraternity House?
SEALS' HOUSE?
GOAT'S HOUSE?
Zebra's House?
LIONS' HOUSE?
SEARCH FOR 'AUTHOR STEPHAN PASTIS' ON FACEBOOK TO VOTE.
...BECAUSE LIVES HANG IN THE BALANCE.
9/5

I am not sure how the actual *Pearls* world is laid out. This was just my best guess. I do, however, know that I made a big error in this strip. See if you can find it yourself, and I'll reveal the answer in the next comment.

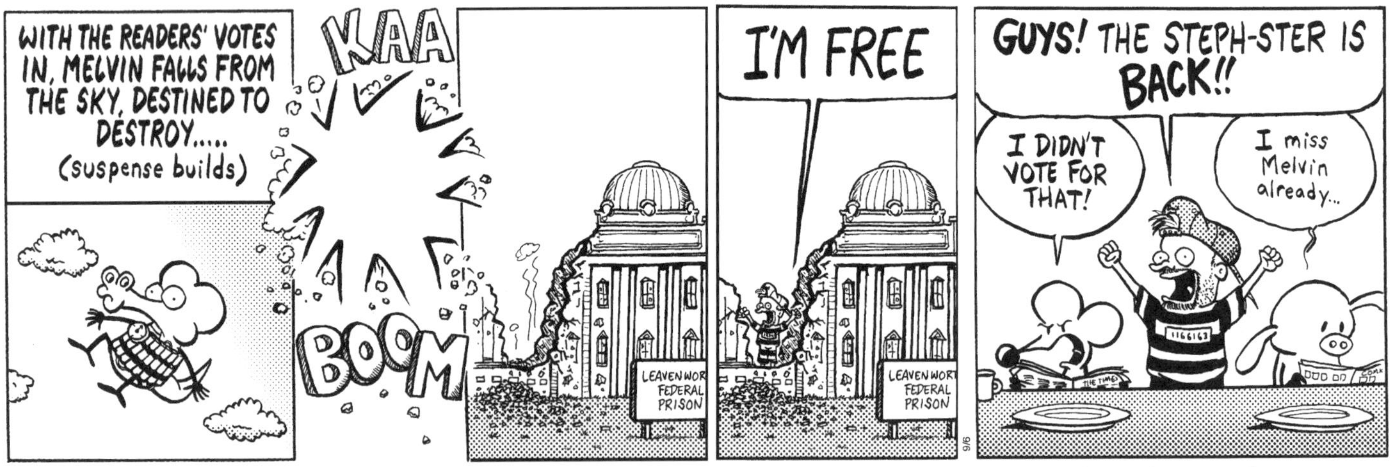
WITH THE READERS' VOTES IN, MELVIN FALLS FROM THE SKY, DESTINED TO DESTROY.....
(suspense builds)
KAA
BOOM
LEAVENWORTH FEDERAL PRISON
I'M FREE
LEAVENWORTH FEDERAL PRISON
9/6
GUYS! THE STEPH-STER IS BACK!!
I DIDN'T VOTE FOR THAT!
I miss Melvin already...

ANSWER TO QUESTION ABOUT LAST STRIP: On the right side is a house marked "Bob and Patty's house." Patty is of course married to Larry.

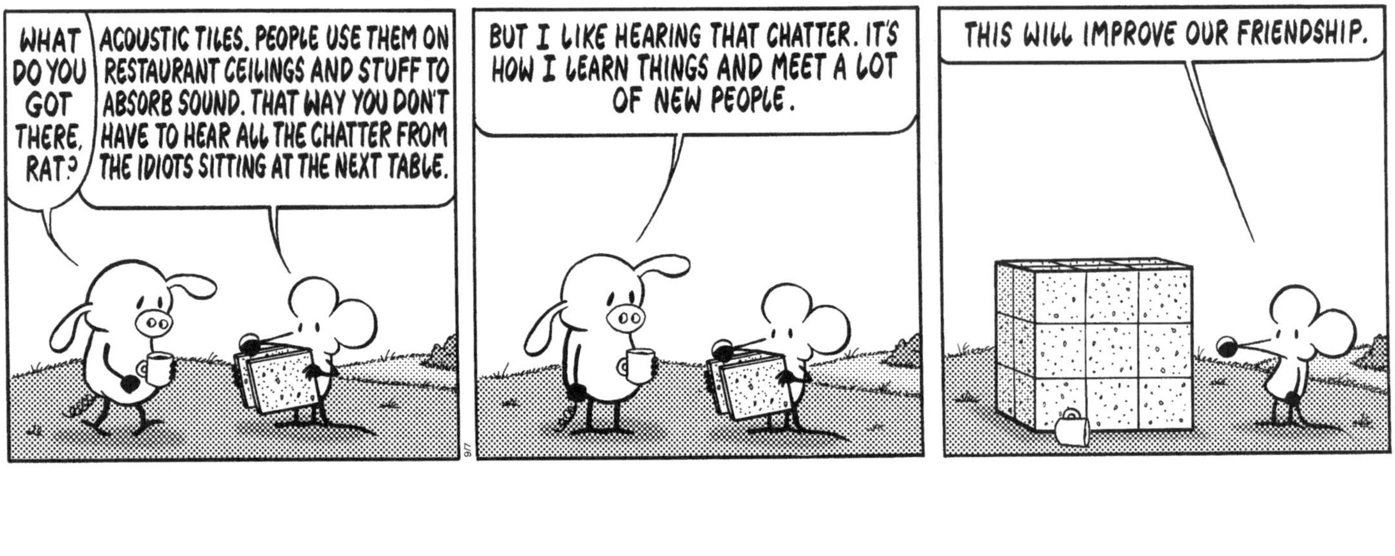
WHAT DO YOU GOT THERE, RAT?
ACOUSTIC TILES. PEOPLE USE THEM ON RESTAURANT CEILINGS AND STUFF TO ABSORB SOUND. THAT WAY YOU DON'T HAVE TO HEAR ALL THE CHATTER FROM THE IDIOTS SITTING AT THE NEXT TABLE.
9/7
BUT I LIKE HEARING THAT CHATTER. IT'S HOW I LEARN THINGS AND MEET A LOT OF NEW PEOPLE.
THIS WILL IMPROVE OUR FRIENDSHIP.

Panel row 1:

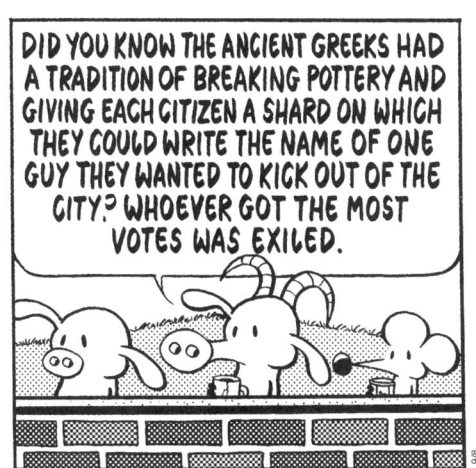

- "DID YOU KNOW THE ANCIENT GREEKS HAD A TRADITION OF BREAKING POTTERY AND GIVING EACH CITIZEN A SHARD ON WHICH THEY COULD WRITE THE NAME OF ONE GUY THEY WANTED TO KICK OUT OF THE CITY? WHOEVER GOT THE MOST VOTES WAS EXILED."
- "IS THAT TRUE?" "YEAH. AND THE GREEK WORD FOR POTTERY IS 'OSTRAKON,' WHICH IS WHERE WE GET THE WORD 'OSTRACIZE'...ISN'T THAT—" *KSCHHHH*
- "THE WORDS, 'THAT BORING GOAT,' WON'T FIT ON MY SHARD."

Everything Goat says here is accurate. Thus, in addition to being humorous, I am also a huge font of knowledge.

Panel row 2:

- "Meow." "Awww...LOOK AT THE CUTE LI'L KITTY...IS HE YOURS?"
- "YES, MA'AM." "Meow. Meow." "DON'T YOU WONDER WHAT SILLY THINGS A LITTLE KITTY WIDDY IS TRYING TO TELL US WITH HIS 'MEOW'S?"
- "Kill. Fat. Lady."
- "YOU MIGHT WANT TO EAT AND RUN, MA'AM." "Meow." "OHHH, I THINK HE LIKES ME."

Panel row 3:

- "I THINK I'M COMPOSED OF TWO SELVES THAT ARE CONSTANTLY AT ODDS WITH EACH OTHER FOR CONTROL OF MY SOUL." "I THINK THOSE TWO SELVES FIGHT IN EACH OF US."
- "EVIL AND EVILER?"
- "EVIL AND GOOD." "GOOD? OH, WE WIPED HIM OUT YEARS AGO."

Rat's statement in the first panel is actually based on a quote by Martin Luther King, Jr.

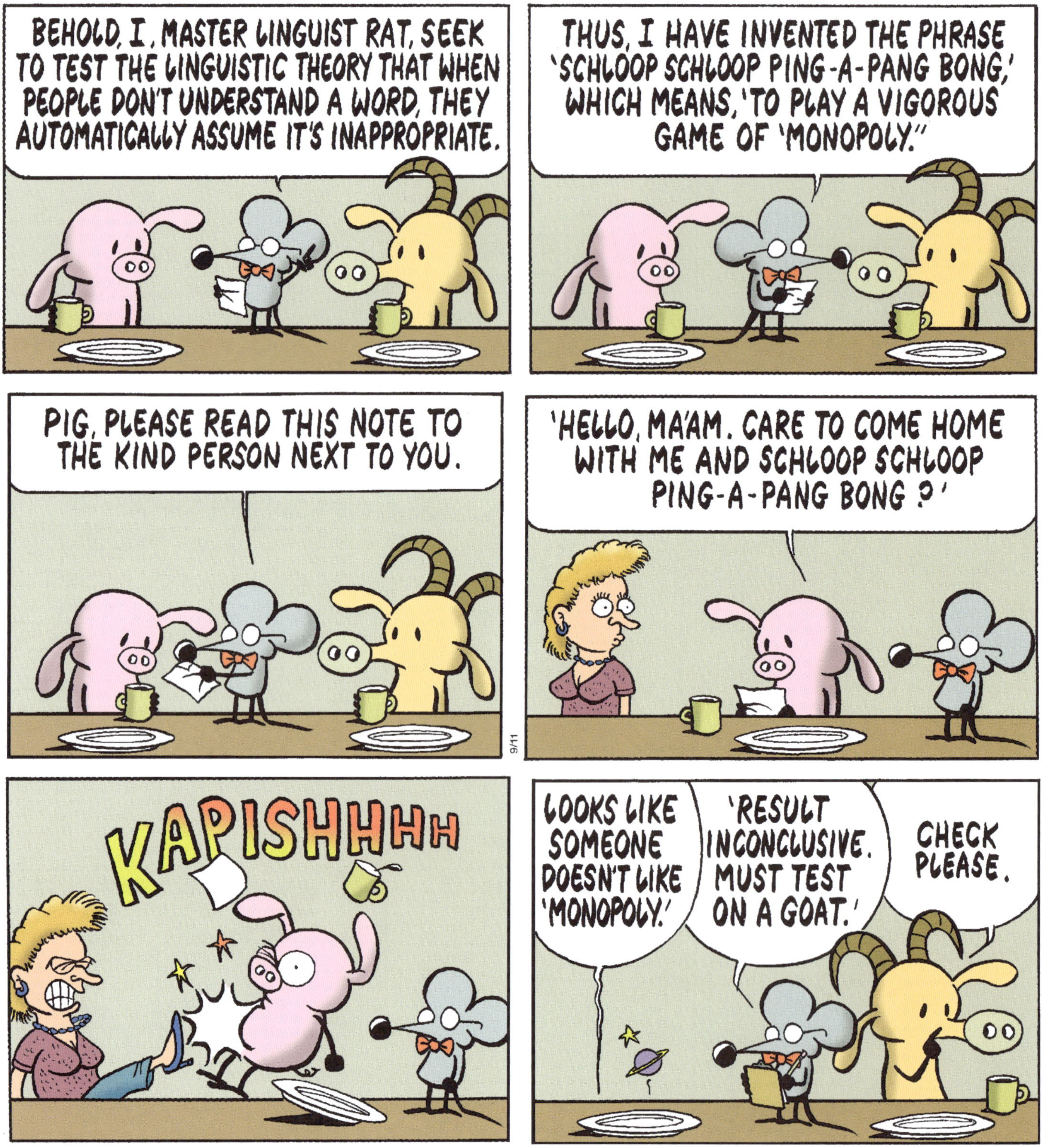
BEHOLD, I, MASTER LINGUIST RAT, SEEK TO TEST THE LINGUISTIC THEORY THAT WHEN PEOPLE DON'T UNDERSTAND A WORD, THEY AUTOMATICALLY ASSUME IT'S INAPPROPRIATE.
THUS, I HAVE INVENTED THE PHRASE 'SCHLOOP SCHLOOP PING-A-PANG BONG,' WHICH MEANS, 'TO PLAY A VIGOROUS GAME OF 'MONOPOLY.''
PIG, PLEASE READ THIS NOTE TO THE KIND PERSON NEXT TO YOU.
'HELLO, MA'AM. CARE TO COME HOME WITH ME AND SCHLOOP SCHLOOP PING-A-PANG BONG?'
9/11
KAPISHHHHH
LOOKS LIKE SOMEONE DOESN'T LIKE 'MONOPOLY.'
'RESULT INCONCLUSIVE. MUST TEST ON A GOAT.'
CHECK PLEASE.

Panel 1:
- DUDE, THIS KEY WEST VACATION WAS MY BEST IDEA EVER.
- YEAH, I— ...WAIT!... I FORGOT MAGIPANTS!

Panel 2:
- YOU WHAT?
- THE PANTS I SLEEP IN...'MAGIC PANTS'... OR AS I CALL THEM, 'MAGIPANTS'...THEY ARE THE COMFIEST SLEEPING PANTS OF ALL TIME! AND THEY ARE BACK AT HOME! ABANDONED!

Panel 3:
- DUDE, SHUT UP. WE JUST FLEW 3,000 MILES TO GET HERE. IT'S NOT LIKE YOU CAN GO BACK AND GET THEM.

Panel 4:
- ARE WE THERE YET?
- AGAIN, SIR, WE JUST TOOK OFF.

I really do have a pair of sweatpants I sleep in that I call "magipants," which is short for "magic pants." Sometimes I even talk to magipants.

Panel 5:
- PIG FLIES HOME FROM VACATION TO GET HIS FAVORITE PAIR OF SLEEPING PANTS.
- MAGIPANTS! MAGIPANTS! YOU'RE UNHARMED!!!

Panel 6:
- I WILL NEVER ABANDON YOU AGAIN! I WILL FLY BACK TO MY VACATION WITH YOU! I WILL WEAR YOU ON MY HEAD IF YOU WANT ME TO! AND I WILL NEVER EVER REMOVE YOU AGAIN!

Panel 7:
- ...SIR, I DON'T CARE WHAT YOU PROMISED YOUR PANTS...YOU'RE TAKING THEM OFF OR I AM.
- PLEASE, SIR. DON'T MAKE ME GET VIOLENT.
- AIRPORT SCREENING — Remove all Headgear

Panel 8:
- DUVAL STREET, KEY WEST, FLORIDA
- THIS IS THE GREATEST TOWN EVER! GREAT BARS! HOT WOMEN! IF ONLY I HAD A SMOOTH WING MAN TO HELP ME WITH THE LADIES...
- SLOPPY JOE'S

Panel 9:
- HIYA, PAL!

Panel 10:
- WHY DOES THE GOD OF LOVE HATE ME SO?
- MAGIPANTS SAYS HELLO.

Sloppy Joe's is a great bar I went to when I was in Key West. I did not, however, wear pants on my head.

Panel 1:
- Rat: HEY, GOAT, I GOT YOUR REPLY TO THAT JOKE I E-MAILED YOU AND I COULDN'T HELP BUT NOTICE YOU USED THAT RATHER HACKNEYED ACRONYM, 'LOL.'
- Goat: YEAH. 'LAUGHING OUT LOUD.' WHY?

Panel 2: CRACK

Panel 3:
- Rat: I'M GONNA STOP THAT ACRONYM ONE INTERNET USER AT A TIME.

I think I can honestly say that I've never used the acronym "LOL." Instead, when someone e-mails or texts me with something funny, I just write, "Hahahaha." Though I never know how many "ha's" are appropriate. Too few "ha's" and your laugh seems too sarcastic. Too many "ha's" and you give the impression that you're falling off your chair with laughter. So I've settled on four "ha's" as just the right amount.

Panel 1:
- Pig: HEY, RAT...WE GOT ONE OF THOSE AUTOMATED PHONE CALLS FROM THE LIBRARY SAYING YOU HAVE AN OVERDUE BOOK...YOU BETTER RETURN IT.
- Rat: WHO CARES, DUDE? IT'S ONE AUTOMATED MESSAGE. LET'S AT LEAST WAIT 'TIL WE GET TWO.

Panel 3:
- Rat: I DON'T THINK WE GET TWO.

Panel 1:
- Rat: HEY, ZEBRA, HAVE YOU MET MY NEW FRIEND, 'MAGIC BUNNY'? IF YOU GIVE HIM A FIVE DOLLAR BILL, HE CAN MAKE IT DISAPPEAR.
- Zebra: OH, YEAH? THIS I GOTTA SEE.

Panel 2: VIVAAAA LAS VEGAS!

Panel 3:
- Rat: GAMBLING IS HIS MAGIC TRICK?
- Zebra: WHO SAID ANYTHING ABOUT MAGIC TRICKS?
- Pig: HOW DID HE *DO* THAT?

I keep hoping to one day include a rabbit as a regular character in the strip. I just haven't found the right personality for him yet.

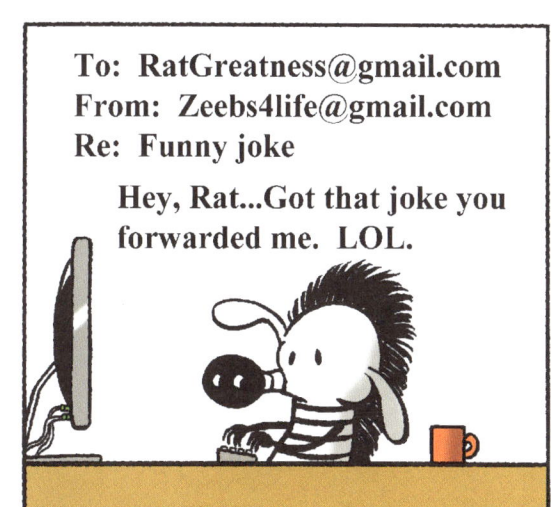

I made sure to establish both of these e-mail accounts on Gmail before doing this strip. I wanted to make sure nobody else had them. Otherwise, some poor guy was going to start getting lots of e-mail about a strange comic strip.

Panel 1:
- WHEN IS IT APPROPRIATE TO SAY, 'I MEANT WELL'?
- I GUESS WHEN YOU DO SOMETHING WITH GOOD INTENTIONS THAT ENDS UP HAVING A BAD RESULT. WHY?
- I CUT DOWN A HUGE TREE TO SEE IF IT WOULD CRUSH YOUR HOUSE AND IT DID. I MEANT WELL.
- PERHAPS YOU DIDN'T HEAR THE 'I MEANT WELL.'

Panel 2:
- HEY, PIG...WHAT ARE YOU DOING HERE? I THOUGHT YOU WERE HANGING OUT WITH YOUR COUSIN LOU TODAY.
- I DID. I TOOK HIM TO THE DINER. HE WAS A BIG HIT. ONE WOMAN SAID HE WAS SO CUTE SHE COULD JUST EAT HIM UP.
- THEN WHAT?
- SHE ATE HIM UP.
- SOME COMPLIMENTS AREN'T THAT COMPLIMENTARY.

I like how nonchalant Pig is about the killing and eating of his cousin right in front of him. Perhaps his penchant for eating pork products clouded his judgment.

Panel 3:
- WHAT ARE YOU DOING, RAT?
- I HAVE STUMBLED UPON A FORM OF COMMUNICATION THAT IS SO CAREFULLY ENCODED I CAN ONLY ASSUME IT WAS ACCIDENTALLY DROPPED HERE BY ALIENS.
- Dw i ddim yn gwybod. Ydw. Mae'n ddrwg gen i.
- THAT'S WELSH.
- DO YOU SUPPOSE THEY COME IN PEACE?

The words in the second panel are actual Welsh words, though I've forgotten what they mean. Just fill in your own definition. The Welsh won't mind.

Panel 1:
- DUDE, YOU'VE BEEN SITTING THERE FOR TEN HOURS JUST WATCHING T.V.

Panel 2:
- I KNOW. MY GIRLFRIEND PIGITA LEFT ME. NOW I JUST FEEL STRANDED AND LOST, LIKE I CAN'T GET UP AND DO ANYTHING EVEN IF I WANTED TO.

Panel 3:
- MUST YOU HIRE A TUGBOAT?

Panel 4:
- I AM SO TIRED OF BOTH POLITICAL PARTIES...I TELL YOU, IN THE NEXT ELECTION I'M GONNA...
- YIP YIP YIP YIP YIP YIP YIP YIP YIP YIP YIP YIP YIP YIP YIP

Panel 5:
- WHAT ARE YOU DOING?
- OBSCURING YOUR VOICE.

Panel 6:
- WHY?!
- YOU BORE ME SO MUCH I FEAR I'LL FALL ASLEEP AND DROWN IN MY SOUP.

Panel 7:
- OH, SO MY CONCERN FOR THE POLITICAL FUTURE OF—
- YIP YIP YIP YIP YIP YIP YIP YIP YIP YIP YIP
- ZZZZZZZZ

Hey, I can draw soup. I just keep expanding my horizons.

Panel 8:
- HEY, GOAT, I'D LIKE TO INTRODUCE YOU TO MY FRIEND, TIMBO THE TORTOISE.
- HOW DO YOU DO?

Panel 9:
- I HAVE NO COMMENT AT THIS TIME.

Panel 10:
- HE'S IN PUBLIC RELATIONS.
- I SEE.
- IF YOU'LL EXCUSE ME, I'M NOW LEAVING TO SPEND MORE TIME WITH MY FAMILY.

I recently sat for a photo shoot where the newspaper photographer asked if I could dress a bit more colorfully. I guess he found my wardrobe selection boring. That made me sad.

Panel 1:
"HEY, RAT, IT'S ME, ZEBRA. YOU SEEN PIG?"
"NOPE. WE WENT TO THE PARK LAST WEEK TO PLAY 'HIDE AND SEEK,' BUT I HAVEN'T DONE ANYTHING WITH HIM SINCE."

Panel 3:
"FOUND YOU."

Okay, bad form again, but I love this strip. Something about the cruelty involved just makes me laugh.

Strip 2, Panel 1:
"HEY, IT LOOKS LIKE THE MACARTHUR FOUNDATION GAVE OUT ITS ANNUAL GENIUS GRANTS, THOSE 23 AWARDS THEY GIVE TO PEOPLE WHO——"

Panel 2:
"SHHHH. WE SHOULDN'T DISCUSS IT."
"WHY NOT? WHO DOESN'T WANT TO TALK ABOUT THE GUYS WHO GOT GENIUS GRANTS?"

Panel 3:
"ONE OF THEM WHO DIDN'T."
"OH, LORD."
"IT'S A @*&#@ SLAP IN THE FACE IS WHAT IT IS."

Strip 3, Panel 1:
"WHAT HAPPENED TO YOU?"
"I GOT FAT."

Panel 2:
"WHY?"
"TO GET RICH... SEE, IF YOU'RE FAMOUS AND YOU GET FAT, ALL YOU HAVE TO DO IS GET UNFAT AND PEOPLE WILL PAY YOU MILLIONS OF DOLLARS TO WRITE A BOOK REVEALING HOW YOU DE-FATIFIED."

Panel 3:
"MAYBE YOU COULD START BY USING REAL WORDS."
"SHUT UP AND BOOK ME ON 'ELLEN.'"
"MORE CHEESE-COVERED FRIED 'TWINKIES', SIR?"

In the last panel, Rat originally told Goat to book him on *Oprah*. But between the time I drew the strip and the time it was to appear in newspapers, Oprah's show ended. Thus, my editor suggested we change it to *Ellen*, which I did. And that's why I'm on the cutting edge of comedy.

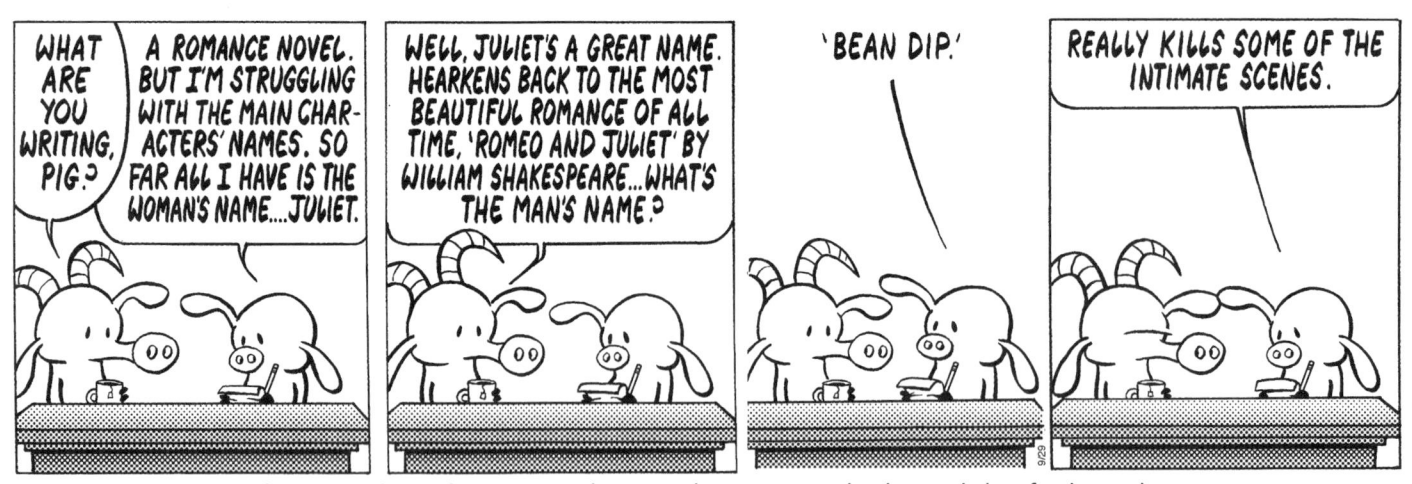

| WHAT ARE YOU WRITING, PIG? | A ROMANCE NOVEL. BUT I'M STRUGGLING WITH THE MAIN CHARACTERS' NAMES. SO FAR ALL I HAVE IS THE WOMAN'S NAME....JULIET. | WELL, JULIET'S A GREAT NAME. HEARKENS BACK TO THE MOST BEAUTIFUL ROMANCE OF ALL TIME, 'ROMEO AND JULIET' BY WILLIAM SHAKESPEARE...WHAT'S THE MAN'S NAME? | 'BEAN DIP.' | REALLY KILLS SOME OF THE INTIMATE SCENES. |

Maybe it's my age (forty-six), but when I recently reread *Romeo and Juliet*, I didn't find it to be romantic. I just found Romeo to be an overdramatic, flighty kid. Fortunately, he dies.

| HEY...WHAT HAPPENED TO YOU? YOU'RE NOT OVERWEIGHT ANYMORE. | YUP. I LOST THE POUNDS. NOW I JUST HAVE TO FINISH THIS BIG BOOK ON HOW I DID IT AND I'LL BE RICH, RICH, RICH. | IS THAT WHAT YOU'RE WRITING NOW? | YEAH...IT'S A THREE HUNDRED PAGE MASTERPIECE CONTAINING ALL MY WEIGHT-LOSS SECRETS. HAVE A LOOK... | I ate less. | I PLAN ON USING A VERY LARGE FONT. |

| HEY, STEPH, WHATCHA READING? | 'POGO' BY WALT KELLY...HE WAS ONE OF THE GREATEST CARTOONISTS EVER. | OHH...EVEN *I* KNOW HIM...HE'S THE GUY WHO CAME UP WITH THAT FAMOUS QUOTE..."WE HAVE MET THE ENEMY AND HE IS... GUS!" | 'US.' | OH... ALWAYS WONDERED WHAT HE HAD AGAINST THAT GUS GUY. |

Walt Kelly's *Pogo* is tremendously respected by most syndicated cartoonists. But I have to admit, I just don't get the strip. I do know, however, that his famous line was, "We have met the enemy and he is us."

| Camille stood on the windswept cliff, the night's stars the only witness to her lonely plight. | One year had passed since her lover boarded the train for the war. | One year of tears and long nights and desperate letters. |

| But as the separation grew, so did the time between his letters, each less passionate than the last. | Now, on the threshold of the reunion to which they had once both counted down the minutes, she stood uncertain that he would return to her at all. |

| And then, at the hour of the darkest night of the soul, a silhouetted figure. | An army uniform. A familiar gait. And a smile illuminated by the stars. | And a joyous call from Camille to her lover... |

"BEAN DIP!"

"SEE, I THINK THE MAN NEEDS A DIFFERENT NAME."

"NAMES ARE SOOOOO HARD."

"CALL THE CHICK 'FRITOS.' THEN YOU'VE GOT SOMETHING."

This strip is a tad problematic because it shows Pig with a very broad vocabulary, which is inconsistent with how dumb he usually is. Maybe he hides his true intellect from us.

Panel 1: OKAY, WE'VE GOT MOTHER'S DAY, FATHER'S DAY, BLACK HISTORY MONTH, GRANDMOTHER'S DAY, EARTH DAY, HISPANIC HERITAGE MONTH, SECRETARY'S DAY AND WOMEN'S HISTORY MONTH. SO.?

Panel 2: SO IS THERE ONE PERSON, THING OR GROUP THAT DOESN'T YET HAVE ITS OWN SPECIAL DAY ON THE CALENDAR? I DON'T KNOW. IS THERE?

Panel 3: GARBANZO BEANS.

Panel 4: GOODBYE. FRIDAY, OCTOBER 7TH IS GARBANZO BEAN DAY!! ONLY FOUR DAYS TO BUY A CARD!

Believe it or not, it turns out there actually *is* a Garbanzo Bean Day, and strangely enough, it is only about two weeks after the date I chose. So in answer to Rat's question, no, there is not one person, thing, or group that is without its own special day on the calendar.

Panel 5: HEY, BOSS MAN...DO WE GET OFF THURSDAY AND FRIDAY THIS WEEK, OR JUST FRIDAY? YOU GET OFF NEITHER. *JOE'S ROASTERY*

Panel 6: I QUIT. *JOE'S ROASTERY*

Panel 7: NO ONE DISRESPECTS GARBANZO BEAN FRIDAY.

Panel 8: HEY, ABOUT YOUR CELEBRATION OF THE GARBANZO BEAN ON FRIDAY, YOU MIGHT WANT TO KNOW THAT HALF THE COUNTRY DOESN'T EVEN CALL THEM THAT. THEY CALL THEM 'CHICKPEAS.'

Panel 9: (silent)

Panel 10: CRACK

Panel 11: IT'S BEST TO DESTROY THESE SPLINTER MOVEMENTS EARLY.

I was sort of surprised I got away with Pig grabbing his garbanzo bikini top and saying, "You don't like my garbanzos?" Score one for the cartoonist.

Note how Goat's clock reads 11:59 in the first panel, and then turns to 12:00 midnight in the third panel. Attention to detail like that makes me the Pulitzer Prize–winning cartoonist that I am.

NOTE FROM EDITORS REGARDING LAST COMMENT: *Stephan Pastis has never won, or even been nominated for, a Pulitzer Prize.*

This one was problematic. I was trying to convey that Rat was talking super fast, but I just couldn't figure out a way to do it with written dialogue. Suggestions welcome.

I bet this was the work of those *Family Circus* punks.

This disturbing clown face was just a doodle in one my notebooks. But I liked the way it looked, and so I turned it into a strip.

Strip 1:

Rat: WHAT ARE YOU DOING, PIG?

Pig: I THREW A MESSAGE-IN-A-BOTTLE IN THE WATER. I'M HOPING IT REACHES SOME FAR-OFF CIVILIZATION, WHO'LL SEND ME A MESSAGE BACK.

Pig: MAYBE THE RING AROUND THE TUB WILL CONTACT YOU.

Rat: WHERE'S A CURRENT WHEN YOU NEED ONE?

I don't do many bathtub jokes because they involve drawing bathtubs. So enjoy this one while you can.

Strip 2:

Rat: HEY, GOAT. WHAT ARE YOU WATCHING?

Goat: YOU'D JUST MAKE FUN OF ME.

Rat: NO I WOULDN'T.

Goat: ALRIGHT, FINE. IT'S FRANÇOIS TRUFFAUT'S '400 BLOWS,' OR 'LES QUATRE CENT COUPS.' THIS AND GODARD'S 'À BOUT DE SOUFFLE' ESTABLISHED 'LA NOUVELLE VAGUE' IN FRANCE.

Rat: YOU'RE A FOO FOO FATFACE.

Goat: THIS IS WHY WE DON'T HAVE THESE DISCUSSIONS.

Rat: OH, SORRY... I SHOULD HAVE SAID '*LE* FATFACE.'

I'm actually a big François Truffaut fan. And *The 400 Blows* is a great movie. So fine, call me a foo foo fatface.

Strip 3:

Pig: LOOK, RAT! IT'S ALICE FROM THE COMIC STRIP 'CUL DE SAC,' AND SHE'S STANDING ON THAT MANHOLE COVER LIKE SHE ALWAYS DOES! HOW COME YOU ALWAYS DO THAT, SWEET L'IL ALICE?

Alice: I'VE TRAPPED THE @☆#@☆#@ 'FAMILY CIRCUS' KIDS IN HERE.

Rat: MY KIND OF GIRL.

Kids: IF YOU LET US OUT, WE'LL SHOW YOU OUR DEAD GRANDPA.

Alice: SHUT YOUR PIEHOLE, JEFFY.

When *Cul de Sac* cartoonist Richard Thompson announced he had Parkinson's disease, I was approached to draw some *Cul de Sac*–inspired artwork that would be auctioned off to benefit the Michael J. Fox Foundation. So I drew the artwork you see here and also ran it as a *Pearls* strip.

HOW WAS DINNER, PIGITA?
GOOD. BUT IF YOU'LL EXCUSE ME, I NEED TO POWDER MY NOSE.
SURE. GO AHEAD.
WHERE YOU GOING?
I JUST TOLD YOU.... TO POWDER MY NOSE.
I THOUGHT YOU WERE GONNA DO IT HERE.
NO, I'M NOT GONNA DO IT HERE.
WHY NOT?
BECAUSE I DON'T WANT TO.
BUT I DON'T MIND A LITTLE POWDER.
IT'S NOT A LITTLE POWDER.
I DON'T CARE IF IT'S A LOT...YOU CAN STILL—
I HAVE TO USE THE @#☆$#@ TOILET!!!
YOU'RE VERY CONFUSING.
10/16

I do not do this. (Okay. Maybe sometimes.)

I'm often asked if I read the comments that people post below my strip where it appears online (pearlscomic.com). And the truth is I don't. I avoid it because I fear it could affect how I write.

For those of you old enough to remember, I think I modeled this character after the rude little girl on the TV show *Little House on the Prairie*. I don't remember the character's name, but I do remember her rudeness.

I think the internet was specifically invented so that bitter people could rip on others with impunity.

Augh! That stupid wall is back! PLEASE, Mr. Gorbachev . . . TEAR . . . DOWN . . . THIS . . . WALL!

Strip 1:

Panel 1: WELL, GOAT, I'VE FINALLY DECIDED... I'M QUITTING COLD TURKEY. / OH, YEAH? WHAT ARE YOU QUITTING? COFFEE? TELEVISION?

Panel 2: COLD TURKEY.

Panel 3: NEVER MIND. / YOU DON'T LISTEN WELL.

Strip 2:

Panel 1: I DATED THE CUTEST GIRL LAST NIGHT. SHE WAS SMART, INTERESTING, SWEET, EVERYTHING. BUT THEN I TOLD A JOKE.

Panel 2: AND WHAT, SHE DIDN'T LIKE IT? / SHE DID.

Panel 3: HAHA SNOOOOORT CACKLE CACKLE HOOO HAWW COUGH COUGH GUFFAWWWEEEE HOOHOO SNOOOOORTT CACKLE CACKLE GUFFAAAAW

Panel 4: BAD LAUGHS: THE GREAT DEAL-BREAKER.

It's sort of odd that Rat dates actual humans. But then again, what in this strip isn't odd?

Strip 3:

Panel 1: LOOKS LIKE THEY FINALLY CAUGHT THAT GUY WHO'S BEEN ROBBING BANKS... IT'S THE BIG HOUSE FOR HIM. / OOOOH... DO YOU SUPPOSE IT HAS A NICE STUDY AND PRETTY CURTAINS?

Panel 2: BOOOOOOOOOO THAT'S ABOUT AS FUNNY AS A 'FAMILY CIRCUS' COMIC

Panel 3: IT'S NOT EVERY DAY YOU SEE A COMIC STRIP HECKLED. / HEY... WHY IS THAT AN INSULT?

I sort of intended that to be a silhouette of the real-life Jeffy (a.k.a. *Family Circus* creator Jeff Keane), although I realized that no one else would recognize that. It just made me laugh to think he would rip on his own work.

109

Panel 1 (strip 1):
Pig: LOOK AT THIS HOTEL ROOM ON THE 'TRAVEL CHANNEL.'...THE BATHROOM HAS A TV! WHAT A GREAT CONVENIENCE! THAT GIVES ME SOME SUPER DESIGN IDEAS FOR OUR HOUSE.

Panel 2:
Rat: TO HANG A FLATSCREEN IN OUR BATHROOM?

Panel 3:
Pig: CLOSE.

If this design idea catches on, I want credit for it.

Panel 1 (strip 2):
Goat: WHY IS IT THAT AT A TIME WHEN MOST PEOPLE ARE HURTING ECONOMICALLY, THERE'S THIS CLASS OF SUPER-RICH PEOPLE WHO ARE DOING BETTER THAN EVER?...WE SHOULD DO SOMETHING ABOUT IT.

Panel 2:
Goat: LIKE WRITE YOUR CONGRESSMAN?
Rat: LIKE PUSH THEM INTO A LAKE.

Panel 3:
Goat: TRY YOUR CONGRESSMAN.
Rat: FINE. WE'LL PUSH HIM IN TOO.

Panel 1 (strip 3):
Goat: WHAT'S GOING ON, PIG?
Pig: THAT PRETTY GIRL ACROSS THE ROOM SMILED AT ME...IT WAS REALLY QUICK AND IT WAS JUST THE CORNER OF HER MOUTH, BUT IT WAS THE MOST BEAUTIFUL MOMENT IN THE HISTORY OF MY LIFE.

Panel 2:
Goat: PIG, SHE HAS A TIC.

Panel 3:
Pig: IS THAT LIKE HAVING FLEAS?
Goat: NEVER MIND.
Pig: BECAUSE IF SO, I THINK OUR LOVE CAN OVERCOME IT.

I think the original idea for this strip was funny (Pig mistaking a tic for a tick). But then I stepped all over the punch line by having three separate speech bubbles in the final panel. That's a sure sign I didn't have enough confidence to let the punch line stand alone.

I recently took my first trip to Philadelphia and was shocked to learn that they had torn down the house of Philadelphia's most famous resident, Benjamin Franklin. So please, all you *Pearls* fans, make sure that every house I ever lived in is carefully preserved for all eternity.

"Heavens to Betsy" has got to be the strangest exclamation ever.

My favorite part about the comics is the fact that you can burn down the characters' house one day, and have it be fine the next. That's what you call "plotline flexibility."

| MY BUDDY BOB GOT KICKED OUT YESTERDAY FOR TWEETING FROM HERE IN THE DINER. | YEAH, A LOT OF RESTAURANTS NOW ASK YOU TO TURN OFF ALL CELL PHONES AND OTHER DIGITAL DEVICES BECAUSE OF THE NOISE THEY MAKE. AND I HAVE TO AGREE. IT'S RUDE TO YOUR FELLOW DINERS. | WHAT'S THAT HAVE TO DO WITH BOB? / FORGET IT. / MIND IF I POST YOUR HUMILIATED FACE ON MY TWITTER PAGE? |

I think the rude part about cell phones in restaurants is not that someone is talking on a cell phone. It's that they're talking so LOUD on a cell phone. I will sometimes turn my body and look straight at the person, as if to say, "Well, if you're going to talk so loud, I might as well pay closer attention."

| HEY, RAT... WHY YOU WEARING AN 'EVEL KNIEVEL' SUIT? / BECAUSE THE CITY INSTALLED LITTLE JUMP RAMPS ON OUR STREET. IF I DRIVE OVER 'EM REALLY FAST, MY CAR ACTUALLY GETS AIR...SO I'M A DAREDEVIL NOW! | THOSE ARE SPEED BUMPS. THEY'RE THERE TO SLOW YOU DOWN. | THEN WHY CALL 'EM SPEED BUMPS? / PLEASE STOP TALKING. / PERHAPS GOAT'S THINKING OF SLOW BUMPS. |

Rat is supposed to be dressed like the famous '70s daredevil, Evel Knievel.

| HOW COME SOMETIMES WHEN I TRY TO DO THE RIGHT THING, EVERYTHING TURNS OUT BADLY FOR ME? | WELL, YOU KNOW, PIG, ACTING WITH HONOR IS ITS OWN REWARD. AFTER ALL, WHAT'S LIFE WITHOUT PRINCIPLES? | FUN. / DON'T LISTEN TO— / I WANT THAT!! |

I had some people argue that this was a racist strip (i.e., I never would have done such a strip in reference to African-American people). I ignored them.

Panel 1:
- I GOT A HIGH-PAYING JOB COMPILING STATS FOR THE GOVERNMENT.
- WELL, THAT'S GOOD. BUT WITH ALL THIS WASTEFUL SPENDING GOING ON, I HOPE IT'S AN ESSENTIAL ONE. WHAT DO YOU COMPILE STATS ON?

Panel 2:
- BANJO FATALITIES.

Panel 3:
- I GIVE UP.
- MIND IF I CONDUCT SOME FIELD RESEARCH?

After this strip ran, a reader directed me to an actual newspaper story where a person really was killed by a banjo. This proves yet again that no matter how strange my story lines, there is something stranger in real life to top them.

Panel 4: RAT, THE GOVERNMENT 'BANJO FATALITY' STATISTICIAN
- WHAT ARE YOU DOING NOW?
- DECIDING WHERE TO PUT THE FIRST 'BANJO FATALITY' CONFERENCE. I'M THINKING IT NEEDS TO BE THE SITE OF THE FIRST KNOWN BANJO FATALITY.

Panel 5:
- WHAT FATALITY WAS THAT?
- BILLY LEE JOE BOB. HE WAS MAKING MOONSHINE WHEN HE TRIPPED OVER HIS HOUND AND IMPALED HIMSELF ON HIS BANJO. BUT WE DON'T KNOW EXACTLY WHERE IT HAPPENED.

Panel 6:
- WHAT'S YOUR BEST GUESS?
- THE FRENCH RIVIERA.

Panel 7:
- NO.
- WELL, BETTER CHECK TO BE SURE.

Panel 8:
- WHAT ARE YOU DOING?
- TRYING TO FIGURE OUT HOW BANJOS CAN BE USED AS PART OF OUR NATIONAL DEFENSE.
- DEPT. OF BANJO FATALITIES

Panel 9:
- WHAT ARE YOU TALKING ABOUT?
- ONCE YOUR DEPARTMENT'S BUDGET IS TIED TO A WEAPONS SYSTEM, IT'S PRACTICALLY SACROSANCT.

Panel 10:
- HOW IN THE WORLD CAN BANJOS BE USED AS A WEAPON?!
- YOU EVER HEARD ONE?

Panel 11:
- I GIVE UP.
- ♪ IF Y'ALL DON'T WANNA HEAR MY BANJY, COME ON OUTTA YER CAVES, TALIBANJY! ♪

Okay, at the risk of offending some of you, I must say that I agree with Rat. I can't stand the sound of banjos.

Panel 1:
- WHAT ARE YOU WRITING, RAT?
- WELL, YOU'VE HEARD OF BOOKS LIKE 'CHEMISTRY FOR DUMMIES'? I'M WRITING MY OWN SERIES... 'CHEMISTRY FOR MORONS.'

Panel 2:
- BUT YOU DON'T KNOW ANYTHING ABOUT CHEMISTRY.

Panel 3:
- THEY WON'T KNOW THE DIFFERENCE.

I actually read *Chemistry for Dummies*. Please. No jokes about me being the appropriate audience.

Panel 4:
- NOW THAT YOU HAVE THIS BIG WALL AROUND YOUR PROPERTY, AREN'T YOU WORRIED YOU COULD LOSE THE KEY TO THE GATE?
- NO. I HAVE A SPARE THAT I KEEP IN A SAFE PLACE.

Panel 5:
- SAFE ENOUGH THAT YOU DON'T THINK THE CROCS CAN GET TO IT?
- YEP.

Panel 6:
- Reech for it, Bob.
- You reech for it, Burt.

Panel 7:
- WHATCHA READING, GOAT?
- A BOOK ON THE PUNIC WARS.

Panel 8:
- OH, THAT SURE IS A NICE WAR.
- WHY IS IT NICE?

Panel 9:
- BECAUSE IF THERE HAS TO BE A WAR, YOU WANT IT TO BE TINY.

Panel 10:
- PUNIC, PIG. NOT PUNY.
- PANIC? OKAY. AUGGHHHH

A dance for Steve (from a Rat who doesn't even *like* to dance).

This was my tribute to Apple founder and visionary Steve Jobs, who died on October 5, 2011.

WELL, I'M OFF TO BUY LOTTERY TICKETS!

PIG, DID YOU KNOW THAT THE ODDS OF YOU WINNING THE LOTTERY ARE WORSE THAN THE ODDS OF YOU GETTING ATTACKED BY A BLACK BEAR AND A POLAR BEAR ON THE SAME DAY?

WHOA. THEN I AM NOT GONNA WASTE THIS ON A LOTTERY TICKET.

GOOD FOR YOU, PIG.

I'M GONNA SPEND IT ON A RIFLE.

NEVER MIND.

DO NOT SHOW FEAR. THEY CAN SMELL IT.

That would really be something to be attacked by a black bear and a polar bear on the same day. Because I don't know about you, but if I got mauled by a black bear, I don't think I'd spend the rest of my day hanging out with a polar bear.

YOU KNOW HOW WHEN SOMEBODY'S REALLY GOOD AT SOMETHING, THEY SAY, 'HE MAKES IT LOOK EASY'?

YEAH. WHY?

YOU MAKE CARTOONING LOOK HARD.

SO MUCH FOR CONSTRUCTIVE CRITICISM.

SOMETIMES I WISH I WASN'T NAMED 'PIG'...IT SEEMS LIKE A WORD THAT CAN SOMETIMES BE USED AS AN INSULT.

I'M A CRAPPIE FISH.

IT'S HARD TO COMPLAIN ABOUT YOUR NAME AROUND A CRAPPIE FISH.

Some people wrote to me to say that while spelled "crappie," the word is actually pronounced "croppie." But the joke doesn't work that way. So screw them and their crappie sense of humor.

Panel 1 (Strip 1):
- Pig: HEY, RAT...LOOK AT THIS GREAT OLD DUSTY TRUNK I FOUND IN THE ATTIC.
- Rat: PUT IT BACK.
- Pig: WHY? WHAT'S IN IT?
- Rat: MY CONSCIENCE. I LOCKED IT AWAY YEARS AGO.
- Narration: WHICH WAS REALLY THE WRONG THING TO DO.
- Rat: PIPE DOWN, YOU PREACHY FUN-KILLER.
- Pig: CAN I GET YOU A SANDWICH??

You might have noticed how elaborately drawn that trunk is. And then you might have noticed how identically drawn it is in each and every panel. And then you might have noticed that you're dealing with a lazy cartoonist who likes to cut and paste.

Strip 2:
- Goat: I HEAR PIG FOUND YOUR CONSCIENCE LOCKED IN A TRUNK IN THE ATTIC.
- Rat: YEAH. AND IF YOU SAY ANOTHER WORD ABOUT IT, I'LL BEAT YOU LIKE A @#*%*#@ RUG.
- Conscience: PROFANITY IS WRONG.
- Rat: THIS COULD GET VERY ANNOYING.

Here I'm so lazy that I came up with a trunk strip where I didn't even have to show the trunk.

Strip 3:
- Caption: RAT CONFRONTS THE CONSCIENCE HE LOCKED AWAY YEARS AGO
- Conscience: LET'S SEE...YOU SKIP CHURCH...GET DRUNK...AND THINK ONLY ABOUT MAKING MONEY...IF THAT'S NOT A PRESCRIPTION FOR SALVATION, I DON'T KNOW WHAT IS.
- Rat: SHUT YOUR FACE. I'VE GOT A PLAN.
- Conscience: LEMME GUESS...YOU'RE GONNA KEEP DOING WHATEVER YOU WANT, BUT ASK FOR FORGIVENESS IN THE SECONDS BEFORE YOU DIE, HOPING LIKE HECK THAT YOUR DEATH DOESN'T ONE DAY CATCH YOU BY SURPRISE.
- Rat: WHO TALKED?
- Conscience: ABOUT TWO BILLION OTHER CONSCIENCES.

And here I'm so lazy that I just reached back to the strip two days prior and cut and pasted the trunk all over again. That takes chutzpah.

STORY UPDATE: Rat has obtained a government job compiling stats on banjo fatalities.

This strip bugs me because the perspective in that fifth panel is all screwed up. The sandbox area is at a very odd angle relative to the sidewalk. If you know anything about perspective, just grab a pen and fix it.

Strip 1:

Pig: WHY IS IT THAT ALL OF US CHARACTERS HAVE TO APPEAR IN THIS COMIC STRIP WITHOUT CLOTHES? WHAT AM I, EYE CANDY FOR MILLIONS OF LASCIVIOUS READERS?

Rat: I GUESS IT'S JUST BECAUSE WE'RE ANIMALS AND WE'RE NOT EXPECTED TO WEAR CLOTHES.

Pig: YEAH, WELL I DON'T CARE. IT MAKES ME MAD. AND THAT'S WHY I'M DOING SOMETHING ABOUT IT.

Stephan: GIVE ME MY PANTS *NOW*.
Rat: COME AND GET 'EM, CARTOON BOY.
Pig: HEY, LOOK! I'M A STEPHAN!

I thought I'd get dinged by my editors for the phallic nature of the plant I'm holding. Shockingly, I did not. Man, I love when I get away with stuff like that.

Strip 2:

Rat: HEY, GOAT, IN AN EFFORT TO IMPROVE THE READERSHIP OF YOUR BLOG, I'VE BEEN STUDYING THE GOOGLE ANALYTICS FOR IT.
Goat: WHAT ARE THOSE?

Rat: A COMPREHENSIVE SERIES OF STATS ABOUT PAGE VIEWS, UNIQUE VISITORS AND HOW VIEWERS FIND YOUR BLOG. ANYWAYS, FROM ALL THAT, I THINK I'VE ASCERTAINED THE PROBLEM.
Goat: WHAT IS IT?

Rat: YOU'RE BORING.

Rat: I SENSE YOU DISPUTE THE DATA.

Strip 3:

Mouse: WHAT ARE YOU READING, GOAT?
Goat: CHEMISTRY. THIS CHAPTER EXPLAINS HOW EACH ELEMENT HAS VALENCE ELECTRONS, WHICH ARE WHAT DETERMINE HOW EASY OR HARD IT IS FOR ONE ELEMENT TO MIX WITH ANOTHER.

Mouse: SOUNDS BORING. HEY, DID YOU GET THIS INVITE TO PIG'S PARTY ON FRIDAY? HE WANTS US TO R.S.V.P. IF WE'RE NOT GOING, WHICH I DON'T THINK I AM.
Goat: YEAH. I DON'T WANT TO GO EITHER, BUT I DON'T KNOW WHAT TO TELL HIM. WHAT ARE YOU GONNA SAY?

Mouse: My valence electrons do not like your valence electrons.

After reading that entire *Chemistry for Dummies* book, I felt the need to show off my vast array of new knowledge. It impressed no one.

Panel 1	Panel 2	Panel 3
Pig: WHAT ARE YOU READING, RAT? **Rat:** CHEMISTRY BOOK. I'M LEARNING ALL ABOUT VALENCE ELECTRONS. THEY'RE WHAT DETERMINE IF ONE ELEMENT CAN BOND WELL WITH ANOTHER.	**Pig:** WHY DO YOU CARE ABOUT THAT? **Rat:** BECAUSE KNOWLEDGE LIKE THAT HAS PRACTICAL USES, YOU MORON. USES I CAN PASS ON TO EVERYONE I KNOW WHO MAY BE DEALING WITH DIFFICULT INTERPERSONAL ISSUES.	**Pig:** IT'S NOT YOU. IT'S YOUR VALENCE ELECTRONS.

Panel 4	Panel 5	Panel 6
Pig: HEY, RAT... I THINK WE NEED TO CHANGE THE GREETING ON OUR ANSWERING MACHINE. **Rat:** WHAT'S WRONG WITH MY OLD ONE?	*(Answering machine:)* LEAVE US THE G#☆@ ALONE.	**Pig:** COULD BE FRIENDLIER.

The answering machine volume at my studio is actually turned down to zero. So when someone calls and leaves a message, I never hear it. It does, however, provide the caller with the comforting illusion that he or she has communicated with me.

Panel 7	Panel 8	Panel 9
Pig: HEY, RAT, DID YOU CHANGE THE GREETING ON OUR ANSWERING MACHINE? **Rat:** YEAH. SEE WHAT YOU THINK.	*(Answering machine:)* HI. YOU'VE REACHED RAT AND PIG. PLEASE LEAVE A MESSAGE AT THE BEEP. BUT IF IT'S LONGER THAN TEN SECONDS, I WILL DRIVE TO YOUR HOUSE AND PUNCH YOU IN THE FACE.	**Rat:** I LIKE TO ENCOURAGE BREVITY.

IF YOU USE YOUR IMAGINATION, YOU CAN SEE LOTS OF THINGS IN THE CLOUD FORMATIONS. WHAT DO YOU THINK YOU SEE, GOAT?	**WELL, THOSE CLOUDS UP THERE LOOK TO ME LIKE THE MAP OF THE BRITISH HONDURAS ON THE CARIBBEAN.**
THAT CLOUD UP THERE LOOKS A LITTLE LIKE THE PROFILE OF THOMAS EAKINS. AND THAT GROUP OF CLOUDS OVER THERE GIVES ME THE IMPRESSION OF THE STONING OF STEPHEN.	**UH HUH... THAT'S VERY GOOD... WHAT DO YOU SEE IN THE CLOUDS, PIG?**
I SEE CHARLIE BROWN.	**STUPID RUNAWAY MACY'S FLOATS.**

The first four panels are an almost word-for-word tribute to my favorite *Peanuts* strip of all time. The strip is from August 14, 1960. In it, Lucy asks Linus and Charlie Brown what formations they see in the clouds. After Linus gives a long and very intellectual response of what he sees ("the profile of Thomas Eakins . . . the stoning of Stephen," etc.), it is Charlie Brown's turn to answer. And all he says is, "I was going to say I saw a ducky and a horsie, but I changed my mind."

Panel strip 1:
- "I HAVE TO GET UP EARLY TOMORROW FOR A JOB INTERVIEW."
- "WELL, LIKE THEY SAY, 'THE EARLY BIRD GETS THE WORM.'"
- "WHAT ABOUT THE WORM? HE GOT UP EARLY AND DIED."
- "I THINK I'LL SLEEP IN."

If I'm allowed to have favorites, I have to say that this is one of my favorite *Pearls* strips.

Panel strip 2:
- "I AM GOING TO DEVELOP A CHARMING SMILE BECAUSE CHARM IS THE KEY TO CONVINCING OTHERS."
- "YOU'VE CONVINCED ME OF *SOMETHING*."
- "DOES SOMEONE NEED TO VISIT THE POTTY?"

This was another one of those strips that just grew out of a doodle in my sketchpad, the doodle here being that image of Rat smiling. I just like the way it looked, so I drew a strip around it.

Panel strip 3:
- "EXCUSE ME, STEPH, BUT MAY I MAKE A LITTLE ANNOUNCEMENT ABOUT A LOOMING SHORTAGE IN ONE OF THE WORLD'S RESOURCES?"
- "I GUESS SO. WHAT IS IT?"
- "YOUNG GIRLS WRITING TEXT MESSAGES MUST STOP USING ALL THE WORLD'S EXCLAMATION POINTS.!!!!"
- "BECAUSE A RAT WITH A @#*☆*@ BLOWHORN WANTS TO USE THEM?"
- "HEY, IT'S OKAY FOR A COMIC STRIP SUPERSTAR."

Panel row 1:

"YOU SPEND TOO MUCH TIME ON THAT iPHONE. IT'S NOT HEALTHY." *Beep Boop Beep*

CRUSH

"THE 'MONTY PYTHON' APP." "WHAT HAPPENED TO ME?"

My homage to one of the most groundbreaking shows in the history of television, *Monty Python's Flying Circus*.

Panel row 2:

"THE KEY TO HAPPINESS IS KNOWING YOUR LIMITATIONS AND ACCEPTING THEM." "I'M SURPRISED TO HEAR YOU SAY THAT, RAT. IT'S A PRETTY MATURE OUTLOOK."

"YEAH...LIKE YOU'RE A POMPOUS IDIOT, AND I ACCEPT THAT."

"WHY DO I HAVE THESE CONVERSATIONS?" "BECAUSE YOU'RE NOT SMART. PLEASE, KNOW YOUR LIMITATIONS."

Panel row 3:

"LOOK AT THOSE TWO PEOPLE TOGETHER. THEY'RE EACH SPENDING THE ENTIRE TIME E-MAILING AND TEXTING ON THEIR iPHONES." "SO?"

"SO IT'S LIKE THEY'RE EACH SAYING TO THE OTHER, 'I'M PHYSICALLY HERE WITH YOU RIGHT NOW, BUT YOU'RE A LITTLE BORING, SO I'D RATHER SPEND TIME WITH OTHER PEOPLE WHO AREN'T HERE.'...... DON'T YOU THINK THAT'S WRONG?"

This strip arose out of an actual complaint to a newspaper about the amount of swearing in *Pearls*. The absurdity of the complaint (at least from my perspective) was that there is not any actual swearing in the strip. Instead, I just use those little squiggles ($&#$, etc.). So I thought I'd have some fun with it by making the reader feel like he was the only one who was interpreting the squiggles as dirty words.

Panel 1:
- HEY, DAD, WHY'S YOUR PAL BOB IN THE BATHROOM?
- He changing clothes. Gonna dress like person from City Planning Deepartment. Tell zeeba he have to tear down beeg wall around property.

Panel 2:
- DOES HE REALLY RESEMBLE A PERSON?
- Peese, son. No eensult us.

Panel 3:
- Yeah. No eensult us.
- Whoa. Reesemblance uncanny.

Woohoo! A mention of someone tearing down that #&%# wall! Oh, please. Oh, please.

Panel 4:
- WHY DO ALL OF THESE OBITUARIES ALWAYS SAY THAT SO-AND-SO 'PASSED AWAY PEACEFULLY'?
- WHAT DO YOU MEAN, 'WHY?'... BECAUSE THE PERSON DIED PEACEFULLY.

Panel 5:
- YEAH, WELL, WHEN I DIE, I'M GONNA GO OUT PUNCHING NURSES AND DOCTORS, JUST SO SOMEONE CAN FINALLY SAY, 'HE PASSED AWAY VIOLENTLY.'

Panel 6:
- WHAT A GOAL.
- BRING IT ON, DEATH!

Panel 7:
- HEY, RAT, I'D LIKE YOU TO MEET MY FRIEND, BOB. HE'S A MECHANICAL ENGINEER. YOU'LL HAVE TO EXCUSE HIM, THOUGH... HE THINKS HE'S MISSING SOMETHING.

Panel 8:
- CHARISMA?

Panel 9:
- MY KEYS.
- MY MISTAKE.
- WOMEN MUST SURE LOVE ALL THOSE PENCILS, BOB.

This strip arose out of a personal challenge. There was a very serious-looking man sitting next to me on a plane who I could tell from his work was some sort of engineer. He had a pocketful of pencils and looked pretty much like the guy you see here. So I wanted to see if I had the courage to write a strip making fun of someone while that someone was sitting right next to me. And so I did. Little did that anonymous man know how much he inspired me.

Strip 1:

Pig: YOU EVER HAVE ONE OF THOSE DAYS WHERE YOUR BRAIN JUST DOESN'T SEEM TO BE FUNCTIONING CORRECTLY?

BONK BONK BONK

Rat: WORKS WITH THE T.V.

Notice how Pig's plate is jostled when Rat bangs on Pig's head. It's subtle little details like that which make *Pearls* the rich tapestry that it is.

Strip 2:

Goat: I GET SO TIRED OF UNMOTIVATED PEOPLE SOMETIMES. HOW CAN SOMEONE HAVE NO PASSION IN LIFE? NO RAISON D'ETRE?

Pig: OH, I'VE GOT SOME OF THAT.

Goat: THAT'S RAISIN *BRAN*.

Goat: IT'S 'A REASON FOR EXISTENCE.'

Pig: NOT REALLY, BUT IT'S A PRETTY GOOD CEREAL.

Strip 3:

Goat: WHERE IS PIG? READING THE NEWSPAPER ON MY iPad. HE WAS FASCINATED THAT THE WHOLE NEWSPAPER WAS ON SUCH AN EASY-TO-READ DEVICE.

Rat: WELL, HOW WAS IT?

Pig: GREAT! I READ THE WHOLE NEWSPAPER!

Rat: WHERE'S THE iPad?

Pig: I USED IT TO LINE MY BIRD CAGE.

Goat: GUESS HE DOESN'T LIKE BIRDS.

Dean, Steve, and Pete are all relatives of mine. I find it funny to name doomed animals in the strip after actual relatives.

Strip 1:

- "DO YOU EVER MEET A PERSON AND KNOW IMMEDIATELY YOU'RE NOT GONNA LIKE THEM?"
- "OH, SURE."
- "YEAH...WHAT IS IT ABOUT CERTAIN PEOPLE THAT TELLS YOU THAT?"
- "THEY'RE BREATHING."
- "MAYBE YOU'RE THE WRONG GUY TO ASK."
- "AND MOUTHS. THEY ALL SEEM TO HAVE MOUTHS."

Whoa. Rat's snout is freakishly long here. It's sad when a cartoonist forgets how to draw his own characters.

Strip 2:

- "WHAT ARE YOU DOING, PIG?"
- "PLANNING A PARTY AT MY HOUSE, BUT I NEED SOME GAMES WHERE PEOPLE CAN WIN PARTY BAGS. DO YOU KNOW ANY GOOD GAMES?"
- "DO THE ONE WHERE YOU PUT PENNIES IN A JAR, AND SEE WHO CAN COME THE CLOSEST TO GUESSING HOW MANY ARE IN THERE."
- "OOH, GREAT IDEA."
- "THREE."
- "YOU ARE REALLY GOOD AT THIS."

Strip 3:

- "BEFORE TODAY'S PERFORMANCE OF 'PEARLS,' WE'D APPRECIATE IT IF ALL OF YOU READERS WOULD PLEASE TURN OFF YOUR CELL PHONES SO AS TO NOT INTERFERE WITH OTHER READERS' VIEWING ENJOYMENT. THANK YOU...."
- "HEY, RAT, WHERE WERE YOU LAST NIGHT?"
- "A MONKEY IN PANTS STOLE MY—"
- *Riiiiiinng Riiiiiing Riiiiiinng Riiiiiing*
- "IT'S THE GUY IN CLEVELAND AGAIN!"
- "USHER, PLEASE REMOVE THE CLEVELAND MAN."
- "HIM AGAIN?!"

The odds are that there was at least one reader in Cleveland whose cell phone rang during the reading of this strip. Imagine how much I temporarily blew his mind.

I should have contacted the creators of a syndicated crossword puzzle and asked them to design a puzzle where the answer to 4-down in that day's puzzle was actually "EVE." That way, Rat really would have been giving away one of the answers to that newspaper's crossword.

Oh, stupid, hard-to-draw wall. Please go away.

If you look really closely, you can see that the woman is holding the very first *Pearls* book. It just had Pig and Rat sitting at the diner and was titled, *BLTs Taste So Darn Good*.

A rare dialogueless strip. To make up for all those wordy ones.

Panel row 1:

- "WHAT ARE YOU WATCHING, GOAT?"
- "'IT'S A WONDERFUL LIFE.' IT'S A CLASSIC CHRISTMAS MOVIE."
- "IS THAT THE ONE WHERE THEY SAY, 'EVERY TIME A BELL RINGS, A PIG GETS BEATEN.'?"
- "THAT'S NOT THE SAYING."
- "PLEASE DON'T RUIN THE FUN."
- "WHY IS THAT A CLASSIC?"

Panel row 2:

- "WHERE WERE YOU GUYS?"
- "SEEING THAT NEW 4D MOVIE."
- "4D? THE FOURTH DIMENSION IS TIME."
- "YEAH. THE MOVIE ENDS BEFORE IT STARTS."
- "NEVER MIND."
- "STRANGE THINGS HAPPEN IN THE FOURTH DIMENSION."
- "LOOK! MY POPCORN'S STILL WARM."

I recently read a quantum physics book that said there are at least *ten* dimensions. That makes me sad. Because even with just three, I get lost driving to the grocery store.

Panel row 3:

- "WHAT ARE YOU DRINKING, STEPH?"
- "A NEW GERMAN BEER. IT'S GREAT."
- "GERMAN?! HA! I DRINK AN ALL-AMERICAN BEER WITH ITS RED, WHITE AND BLUE LABEL AND ITS ALL-AMERICAN ADS FILLED WITH AMERICAN FLAGS AND AMERICAN BARBECUES AND AMERICAN BASEBALL!!"
- "THAT BEER YOU'RE HOLDING IS NOW OWNED BY A EUROPEAN COMPANY."
- "I KNEW THAT."

This was supposed to be a reference to Budweiser, which was sold to a Belgian company in 2008.

Panel 1:
- "You hope to accomplish a lot in life, right?"
- "Sure. Why?"

Panel 2:
- "Because I just figured out that with you being 43 years old, and the average life expectancy for a man being 76 years old, your life is at least 56 percent over."
- "So?"

Panel 3:
- "So if your life is a football game, you're well into the third quarter and down 20 points."

Panel 4:
- "Are you done?"
- "Lemme guess.. you're banking on a miraculous fourth quarter comeback."
- "THROW A HAIL MARY, STEPH!"

Now I am forty-six. So my life is at least *60 percent* over. That makes me even sadder than the ten-dimension thing.

Panel 1:
- "What are you writing, Pig?"
- "A bucket list of all the things I'd like to do before I die."

Panel 2:
① Stand on it.
② Put it on head.
③ Roll it down street.

Panel 3:
- "You know, things on your bucket list don't have to involve buckets."
- "Whoa. Now that broadens things."

Panel 1:
- "Hey, Pig, what's wrong?"
- "Ohh, Zebra... I've been hearing voices."

Panel 2:
- "Really?"
- "Really."

Panel 3:
- "Well, look...it's not the end of the world. We'll get you help...a good psychologist."
- "How will that make the couple next door stop fighting?"

Panel 4:
- "*Those* are your voices?"
- "Hey...what can he do about their barking dog?"

We had a neighbor that was so loud that one day, I just opened the window and yelled, "DUDE, SHUT THE #%*# UP!!" As those were the first words I'd ever spoken to him, it did not get our relationship off to a good start.

"Well now, there's a constellation you don't see every day."

For Bil Keane, 1922-2011

This was my tribute to *Family Circus* creator Bil Keane, who died on November 8, 2011. He was always a terrific sport about all of my *Family Circus* parodies, and even had one of them hanging on his wall at home. He was a great man, and I'll miss him.

I thought this strip was too weird, even for me. So I almost didn't run it at all. Finally, I decided to go ahead and run it, but hide it in the week after Christmas, when fewer people read the comics.

The wall that haunts me. Back once again.

I love that I got away with having Goat point at Rat and say, "Your little thingie there is called a shuttlecock." But who could complain? The things you hit in badminton are in fact called "shuttlecocks." Oh, the fun I have.

Showing someone getting shot in a comic strip can get you into a lot of trouble with certain readers and editors. Particularly when it's a fairly realistic looking gun and a human getting shot. So I hid this strip in the week after Christmas also.

This was, indeed, the tenth anniversary of *Pearls*, which first appeared in the *Washington Post* on December 31, 2001.

Elly Elephant was sick of Henry Hippo.

So she sat in her kitchen and tried to envision her dream man.

"I will take this empty basket and put in one avocado for each trait I want in a man."

So she put in one avocado for sensitivity, and one for handsome, and one for adventurous.

"And I want him to be dependable," she said, putting in another avocado. But when she did, out fell adventurous.

"Well, he at least needs to be non-superficial," she said, adding another avocado. But out dropped handsome.

"Okay, he can't be needy," she said, squeezing in another. But out fell sensitive.

"The basket can't hold all the avocados," Elly cried in despair. "I'll simply have to learn to be happy with the few avocados I have."

Which was none because Henry Hippo turned them into guacamole.

OH, THIS IS AN UPLIFTING TALE.

"SO REMEMBER, PEOPLE, BE HAPPY WITH THE CRAPPY PARTNER YOU HAVE."

I WILL STRIVE TO BE ALONE FOREVER!

A woman wrote to me to say that this was her favorite *Pearls* strip. But then she added this rather odd compliment: "You are the reason I still get the paper. Well, you and the obituaries."

Panel 1 (strip 1):
- "GUARD DUCK STARTED PLAYING BINGO WITH THE SENIORS AT THE RETIREMENT CENTER."
- "WHY BINGO?"
- "DOCTOR SAID HE HAS HIGH BLOOD PRESSURE. IT'S SUPPOSED TO HELP HIM RELAX."
- "THAT'S GREAT. HOW'S HE DOING WITH IT?"
- "NO, I DO NOT WANT TO FORM A BINGO ALLIANCE."

One week after I show a man getting shot with a gun, I show an old woman being threatened with an RPG. I blame my poor upbringing.

Strip 2:
- "DO YOU REALIZE THAT IN 1985, THERE WERE ONLY 13 BILLIONAIRES IN THE U.S., AND TODAY THERE ARE MORE THAN 1,000? SO WHILE MOST OF US STRUGGLE, THERE'S THIS CLASS OF THE SUPER RICH WHO'VE THRIVED."
- "THAT'S NOT FAIR. WE NEED TO CHANGE THAT."
- "I AGREE. BUT HOW?"
- "BY JOINING THAT CLASS."
- "I THINK YOU'RE MISSING THE POINT."
- "LET ME BE ONE OF YOU, RICH PEOPLE!"

Strips like this anger people, though I'm never quite sure why. As one woman wrote, "You will join *Doonesbury* if this keeps up. I haven't read it in years."

Strip 3:
- "THE CROCS ARE ASKING THE CITY TO TEAR DOWN YOUR WALL ON THE GROUND THAT IT POSES A DANGER TO CHILDREN."
- "HOW DO THEY FIGURE THAT?"
- "THEY SAY A HELPLESS CHILD COULD CLIMB ON TOP AND SUFFER A TRAGIC FALL."
- "BUT THAT'S NEVER HAPPENED. AND THEY HAVE NO PROOF IT EVER WOULD."
- "Why me got wear funny costume, Bob?"
- "Shut mouf and walk closer to edge, Burt."

Panel 1:
- Pig: LOOK WHAT I BOUGHT, RAT...IT'S THE 'MOUNTED BUFFALO HEAD OF REGRET.'
- Rat: WHAT'S THE REGRET?

Panel 2:
- NOT DUCKING.

Panel 3:
- IT'S REALLY LIMITED HIS OPTIONS.

For a while, I was writing *Pearls* in an old Victorian house that doubled as a cafe. And the room I wrote in had this huge buffalo head hanging on the wall. It was inevitable that it would make its way into the strip.

Panel 4:
- Pig: HEY, RAT, I'M TRYING TO SET UP THAT POKER GAME YOU ASKED FOR, BUT I DON'T KNOW WHO TO INVITE.
- Rat: WHO CARES? WE JUST NEED PLAYERS. ASK ANYONE WITH ARMS THAT CAN HOLD CARDS.

Panel 5:
- THAT HURTS.

Panel 6:
- TRY TO BE MORE SENSITIVE AROUND MR. BUFFALO HEAD.

Panel 7:
- Goat: WHAT'S THE MATTER, PIG?
- Pig: MY STUPID COMPUTER. IF I DON'T USE AN ANTI-VIRUS PROGRAM, I GET SOME RUSSIAN-MADE VIRUS ON MY COMPUTER THAT STEALS MY CREDIT CARD NUMBER.

Panel 8:
- Pig: BUT IF I DO USE AN ANTI-VIRUS PROGRAM, IT SLOWS MY COMPUTER DOWN TO A CRAWL AND INTERRUPTS EVERYTHING I DO WITH STUPID MESSAGES.

Panel 9:
- Goat: YEAH, BUT WHAT CAN YOU DO?
- Pig: I E-MAILED MY CREDIT CARD NUMBER TO THE RUSSIANS.

Panel 10:
- IT'S A BIG TIME-SAVER.

What are you supposed to be? Vito Corleone. I'm going to a mob costume party.	**A mob costume party?** Yeah. And this is a statue of Jimmy Hoffa. Guard Duck made it for me. I bring one every year.
What for? At the end of the party, the mobsters blow it up. There's a little fuse in his head. But I think we need to change the design. **Why is that?**	Because people are always re-doing the fuse to make it shorter. That way it blows up right when they light it. **But that's not safe.**
I know. That's why I'm changing it. **What are you gonna do?**	I'm gonna make them a Hoffa they can't re-fuse.

Wow, this is a convoluted premise. And I'm proud of that.

There's something so liberating about writing the sentence, "Shut your face, Grover."

Look how detailed Oscar's trash can is here, and how plain it is in the prior strip. Clearly, I was feeling much more ambitious here.

142

For those that don't know, Mr. Rogers opened his show by singing, "Won't you be my neighbor?" Rat's version is slightly different.

Yeah. It's back.

WOOOOHOOOOOO!! TAKE THAT, YOU STUPID, TIME-CONSUMING, HAND-TIRING PREMISE!!!!

Panel 1:
YOU EVER NOTICE HOW SOME OF THE OLDER COMIC STRIPS ALWAYS HAVE A WIDE-EYED OPEN-MOUTHED GUY IN THE LAST PANEL?

YEAH. IT'S A VISUAL CUE SO THE READER KNOWS HE'S JUST READ THE PUNCHLINE.

Panel 2:
WHY DON'T YOUR STRIPS HAVE THAT?

I DON'T KNOW... I GUESS I HOPE THE JOKE IS WELL WRITTEN ENOUGH THAT THE READER DOESN'T NEED AN OBVIOUS CUE LIKE THAT.

Panel 3:
!

Panel 4:
GET RID OF HIM.

WHOA... NOW I GET THIS STUPID STRIP.

ZOINKS!

If you ever look back at the old, pre-1950 comic strips, you'll find that this is mostly true. It really wasn't until the comic strip *Peanuts* that cartoonists stopped doing this.

Panel 1:
WHAT HAPPENED TO YOU, STEPH?

I FLEW FROM L.A. TO OAKLAND AND THE AIRLINE LOST MY LUGGAGE. IT HAD ALL MY CLOTHES, MY HAT, MY CONTACT LENSES. THEY HAVE NO IDEA WHERE IT IS.

Panel 2:
OH, NO, STEPH... WAS THERE ANYTHING IN THERE YOU CAN'T REPLACE?

Panel 3:
WHERE THE G☆#☆ AM I?

Welcome to ALBANY NEW YORK

LUGGAGE CAROUSEL 3

This was based on a true event. Southwest Airlines lost my luggage on a flight from Los Angeles to Oakland and it somehow ended up in Albany, New York.

Panel 1:
STEPH! STEPH! RAT WAS IN YOUR LOST LUGGAGE! HE SNUCK INSIDE BECAUSE HE DIDN'T WANT TO PAY FOR AIRLINE TICKETS! NOW HE'S LOST! WHAT ARE WE GONNA DO?!

Panel 2:

Panel 3:
WE SHOULD TRY TO GET HIM BACK, STEPH.

SHHHH. SAVOR THE MOMENT.

| HELLO? | HI. THIS IS SOUTHWORSTERLY AIRLINES. WE'VE FOUND YOUR LUGGAGE WITH THE RAT INSIDE. HE'S UNHARMED, BUT A LITTLE ANGRY. WHERE WOULD YOU LIKE IT SENT? | | YAKUTSK, SIBERIA — I'LL KILL HIM IF IT'S THE LAST THING I DO. |

The only reason I know there is a place called Yakutsk is because it's on the Risk board and I invade it frequently.

| HI, PIG. I'M GONNA BE LEAVING THE STRIP FOR A WHILE. RAT JUST GOT BACK FROM SIBERIA AND I THINK HE'S A LITTLE UPSET WITH ME FOR SENDING HIM THERE. | OHH, HE JUST TALKS TOUGH. HE'LL GET OVER IT. | YEAH, YOU'RE PROBABLY RIGHT. BUT IT'S STILL A GOOD EXCUSE TO TAKE A VACATION. | OKAY, WELL IF YOU'RE REALLY GONNA GO, COME DOWN HERE AND GIMME A BIG HUG. | WOOSH WOOSH WOOSH THWACK | IT'S NICE TO BE IN A STRIP SO FILLED WITH LOVE. |

Medieval weaponry is instant comedy.

| HEY, PIG, WHERE WERE YOU THIS MORNING? | I HAD TO GO WITH PIGITA TO THE DOCTOR'S OFFICE. SHE'S HAVING TROUBLE DRINKING MILK. | WHAT'D THE DOCTOR SAY? | HE SAID SHE HATES PEOPLE WHO ARE MISSING TOES. | THE TERM IS 'LACTOSE INTOLERANT.' | YEAH. AND TO ME, THAT'S RACIST. |

STORY UPDATE:

Stephan Pastis is on the run from Rat, who is upset at Stephan for shipping him to Siberia. Today, Stephan's travels bring him to Kansas City, Missouri.

STEPHAN PASTIS! WHAT BRINGS YOU TO K.C.?

HI, JOHN GLYNN, V.P. OF MY NEW COMIC STRIP SYNDICATE. I'VE JUST COME FOR A LITTLE VISIT. I WAS WONDERING IF I COULD STAY WITH YOU.

SURE THING, STEPHSTER... WELCOME TO THE SYNDICATE!

GEE, THANKS, JOHN. AND TO SHOW MY APPRECIATION, I'VE BROUGHT YOU A 'STEPHAN PASTIS' MASK. I THOUGHT IT'D BE FUNNY. HERE, TRY IT ON...

KATHUNK

I DON'T THINK I WANT TO BE STEPHAN ANYMORE.

SORRY, SIR. YOU LOOKED LIKE ANOTHER ROTUND IDIOT I KNOW.

So John Glynn really is the vice president of my new comic strip syndicate, Universal Uclick. And his office really does look like that. And yes, all he does all day is sit at his desk and scarf hot dogs and guzzle beer. *(Lawyer's Disclaimer: John Glynn does not spend his entire day scarfing hot dogs and guzzling beer.)*

STORY UPDATE
Stephan Pastis has returned from Kansas City convinced that Rat's attack upon John Glynn has dissipated any anger Rat harbored toward him. Stephan now feels safe enough to enjoy a meal out with Pig and Goat.

In the last episode of *The Sopranos*, the person who was most likely Tony's killer is wearing a Members Only jacket and is sitting at the counter in the background. So if you look closely here, you'll see that Rat is sitting at the counter wearing a jacket.

I can't remember where I first heard a person's rear end referred to as a "badonkadonk," but it really made me laugh, so I thought I'd try to use it in the strip.

STORY UPDATE: Someone has taken a photo of a drunken Larry in a bar greeting a zebra with the crocodiles' sacred badonkadonk greeting, which involves one party rubbing his buttocks (badonkadonk) against that of the second party.

ME GOTTA KEEL PERSON WHO HAVE PHOTO BEFORE LARRY WHOLE LIFE RUINED!!!

YOU got photo, Larry. Was taken on you iPhone.

Larry iPhone?? Den me juss delete before anyone see!!

Dat GREAT idea.

If you no had posted on Facebook.

IT'S HILARIOUS. A FRIEND SENT IT TO ME.

CURSE YOU, SOSHILL MEEDIA!!

STORY UPDATE: A drunken Larry was photographed rubbing his badonkadonk against that of a zebra, which Larry then posted on Facebook. Larry returns to his croc fraternity in the hopes that the whole matter has quietly gone away.

Hey, guys... Want have beer?

It hasn't.

Mebbe me drink by myself behind tree.

This is the same fraternity house that is on the cover of the *Pearls* collection, *Da Brudderhood of Zeeba Zeeba Eata*. I think this is the only time I've ever drawn it in the strip itself.

HEY, RAT, I'D LIKE YOU TO MEET MY FRIEND, JIM. HE'S A PRO GOLFER WHO PLAYS ON ALL THE WORLD'S GREAT COURSES... AUGUSTA, PEBBLE BEACH... YOU NAME IT.

OH?... HOW'D YOU SCORE AT K-TOPE?

K-TOPE?

KIDTOPIA PUTT-PUTT GOLF COURSE.

AFRAID I HAVEN'T PLAYED.

MAYBE WE SHOULD LEAVE.

HA! SOUNDS LIKE SOMEONE FEARS THE HANSEL AND GRETEL PAR 3 FIFTH!

I do not fear the Hansel and Gretel fifth hole at my local miniature golf course. But I do fear the volcano-shaped fourth hole that recently made me lose to my son Thomas. You have to hit the stupid ball onto this high mound, but the ball just goes up one side and then back down the other side. It's not fair. And now I'm angry.

You can't throw a beer can at a blind guy without upsetting a few readers. And upset they got. As one reader wrote to her Florida newspaper, "I believe Stephan Pastis owes an apology to all handicapped people, and should use common sense in his comic strip. He should not condone violence and ridicule that will be read by children and young adults."

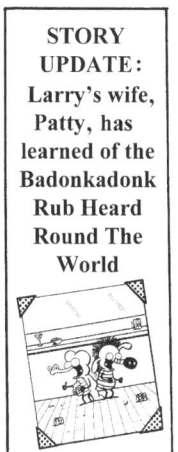

I actually created this Twitter account for the purpose of this one strip.

If you look really carefully at the background of the second panel, you'll see two signs, "Bar" and "Nudes." Thought I'd sneak those into Mr. Rogers' neighborhood.

151

MR. RAT'S NEIGHBORHOOD
HI, BOYS AND GIRLS... I THINK IT'S TIME FOR SOME MAKE-BELIEVE... OH, TROLLEY... COME TAKE US TO THE LAND OF MAKE-BELIEVE....

DING DING
DING DING

THIS IS HOW *I* GO TO THE LAND OF MAKE-BELIEVE, BOYS AND GIRLS.
CUT

MR. RAT'S NEIGHBORHOOD
HI, BOYS AND GIRLS. THIS IS KING FRIDAY AND QUEEN SARA. KING FRIDAY IS USUALLY A HAPPY KING. BUT TODAY HE IS SAD. WHY? BECAUSE THE ARAB SPRING HAS THREATENED DESPOTIC MONARCHS EVERYWHERE.

OH, NO, KING FRIDAY... IT'S JIHAD JERRY.
POP POP POP

OH, WELL... TRY TO HAVE A DEMOCRATIC FORM OF GOVERNMENT, JERRY.
YOU... PUT ON BURKA.

This made people angry for a variety of reasons. One reader wrote, "Guns have no place in comic strips. I have written to my newspaper asking them to drop *Pearls Before Swine* because of your use of guns." Another wrote, "Jihad Jerry? Really? . . . What you printed today is a horrible caricature of Islam." And yet another commented, "You must be getting some serious crap over the content of this week's strips." He was correct.

MR. RAT'S NEIGHBORHOOD
HI, BOYS AND GIRLS. TODAY WE'RE GONNA LEARN ABOUT REVOLUTION, LIKE THE ONE JIHAD JERRY JUST PULLED OFF IN MR. RAT'S NEIGHBORHOOD.

Burkas Required

AS YOU MAY NOTICE, I'M NOW DRESSED A LITTLE DIFFERENT. BUT DON'T WORRY, BOYS AND GIRLS. OTHER THAN THAT, EVERYTHING ELSE IN MR. RAT'S NEIGHBORHOOD WILL BE JUST LIKE IT ALWAYS WAS. ISN'T THAT RIGHT, MR. TROLLEY?

Die Imperialist Dogs

DING! DING!
HEY, TROLLEY, SELL THIS OIL TO MR. McFEELY AT EXORBITANT PRICES.
Bad news. Meester McFeely taken hostage by rival sect.

One reader with an entirely different perspective on these strips commented, "I think it is a nice start for children to begin to understand what the Western World is up against." And here I thought I was just making fun of Mr. Rogers.

ALL I DO IS WORRY.
ABOUT WHAT?
THINGS THAT HAVE HAPPENED. THINGS THAT HAVEN'T HAPPENED. THINGS THAT MIGHT HAPPEN.
WHAT GOOD DOES THAT DO?
BECAUSE IF I DON'T WORRY, LIFE'S BAD STUFF WILL SNEAK UP ON ME. WORRYING IS MY WAY OF SAYING '@★#$% YOU, LIFE... YOU WON'T SURPRISE ME.'
BUT YOU BELIEVE LIFE IS BAD ANYWAY. SO WHY WORRY?
MAYBE YOU'RE RIGHT.
YEAH. SO CLOSE YOUR EYES AND RELAX.
RELAX.
2/5
CRACK
I'VE BEEN WAITING TEN YEARS TO DO THAT.
NEVER STOP WORRYING.

Panel 1:
"HEY, RAT, I HOPE YOU DON'T MIND, BUT I HAVE A COUPLE FRIENDS COMING OVER. THEY'RE ROADRUNNERS."
"ROADRUNNERS ARE GREAT, DUDE. THEY'RE RIDICULOUSLY FAST. I'D LOVE TO JUST WATCH HOW THEY MOVE."

Panel 3:
"THAT'S DISAPPOINTING."

Panel 4:
"DO YOU EVER THINK THAT AS A SOCIETY WE'VE GROWN SOFT? THAT RATHER THAN RELY ON OUR GOD-GIVEN ABILITIES, WE NOW JUST RELY ON SOMEONE OR SOMETHING ELSE TO GIVE US A BOOST?"
"I DON'T THINK THAT'S TRUE. I THINK—"
BEEP BEEP

Panel 5:
"SPARE A BUCK FOR TWO TIRED ROADRUNNERS?"

Panel 6:
"THAT'S DISTURBING."
"MONEY, PLEASE."

After I started drawing these roadrunner strips, I realized there was no way they could become regular characters. The Segway was just too darn hard to draw. Which brings up Stephan's First Rule of Drawing: Avoid anything with wheels.

Panel 7:
"HEY, IF IT'S NOT MY GOOD FRIEND, JEFF THE CYCLIST! HOW ARE YOU, JEFF?"
"BETTER THAN YOU. AND THAT IS WHY I SHOW MY SUPERIORITY BY RIDING MY BIKE RIGHT IN FRONT OF YOUR CAR, INSTEAD OF IN THE BIKE LANE."

Panel 8:
"GOSH, JEFF, I WISH YOU WOULDN'T DO THAT BECAUSE—"
"EAT MY SPANDEX GREATNESS, FATTY McFAT FAT!!"

Panel 9:
"AND THAT'S WHY I TRY TO RUN THEM OVER."
"JEFF, YOU'RE ON MY BREAKFAST."
"I STAMP OUT YOUR FATTENING FOOD AS A FAVOR TO YOU!!"

This generated more angry complaints than anything I had drawn in years. And it wasn't for the portrayal of the cyclist. It was for Rat's line in the final panel. Little did I know I had inadvertently hit upon the most sensitive subject matter in the world of cycling—drivers who purposely try to scare cyclists by driving too close to them or even running them off the road. I was vilified on cycling message boards, newspaper articles, you name it. And the e-mail I received contained the most outrage I had seen since my Ataturk strip that angered Turks. One example: "Yesterday was the first time in three years I was honked at and ran off the road for occupying one-third of a traffic lane (no bike lane). Now I ask you, did this person read your cartoon and suddenly feel empowered to 'take back the road'? Probably not, but if he did and I was injured that would have been my blood on your hands." So if you're keeping score at home, the two most humorless groups in the world are radical Turks and cyclists in tight pants.

No Segway riders complained about this strip. Apparently, they're slightly more easy-going than cyclists.

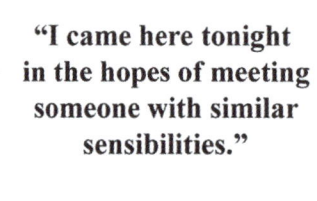

Elly Elephant was tired of staying home Friday nights.

So she went to a bar.

"Hello," she said to the hippo sitting on the bar stool next to her. "I am Elly Elephant."

"My interests are 19th century romantic poetry, South American birds and the work of historian Robert Caro."

"I came here tonight in the hopes of meeting someone with similar sensibilities."

"Oh, silly me," said Elly. "All I've done is go on oafishly about myself. I'm sure you have much more erudite things to say."

"Nice rear."

Elly Elephant beat the erudite hippo with his own bar stool.

WAP WAP WAP

YOU KNOW, MOST ROMANCE NOVELS HAVE HAPPY ENDINGS.

YEAH... I'M MAKING UP FOR THAT.

HER REAR *IS* RATHER ATTRACTIVE.

I snuck myself into the fourth panel. You can just see the back of me.

156

Panel 1:
- "Hey, Jeff the cyclist. How are things?"
- "Intense. I have to put in long hours training for my next race. My wife and kids don't seem to understand."

Panel 2:
- "I didn't know you had a wife and kids. What are their names?"

Panel 3: (silent)

Panel 4:
- "You should spend more time with your family, Jeff."
- "Wait... I think one of them is a 'Betty.'"

The cyclists were oddly quiet in response to this one. I take that as an admission that they spend too little time with their family.

Panel 1:
- "Do you think there's an element of fraud in many protests? That some people rail against the very thing they exemplify?"
- "I don't think that's true."

Panel 2: FIGHT LAZINESS

Panel 3:
- "I've changed my mind."
- "Exercise, people!"

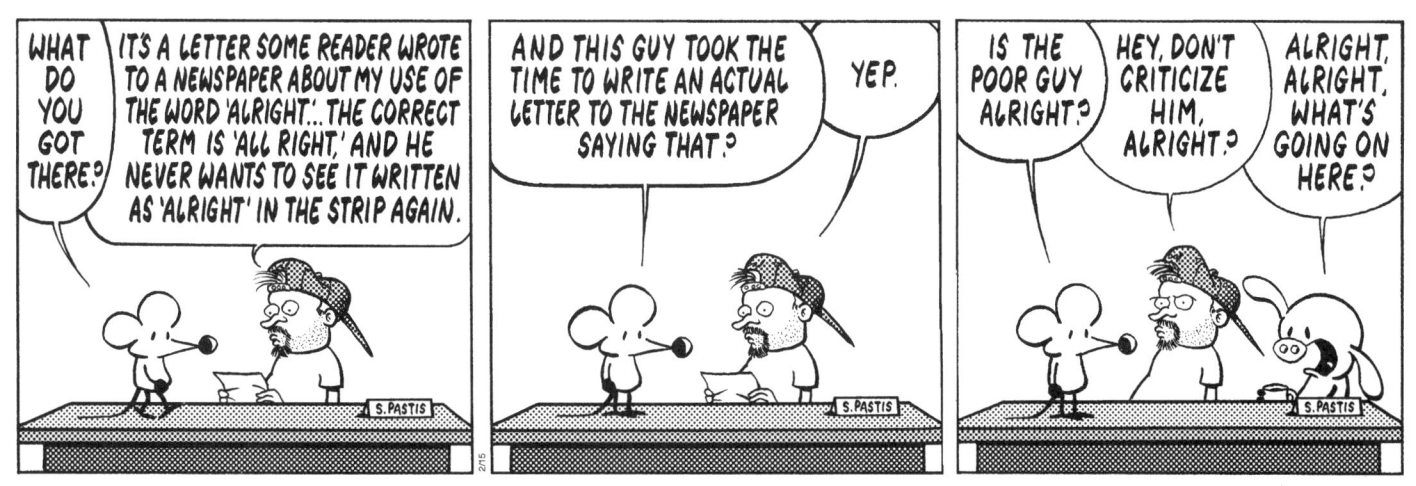

Panel 1:
- "What do you got there?"
- "It's a letter some reader wrote to a newspaper about my use of the word 'alright'... The correct term is 'all right,' and he never wants to see it written as 'alright' in the strip again."

Panel 2:
- "And this guy took the time to write an actual letter to the newspaper saying that?"
- "Yep."

Panel 3:
- "Is the poor guy alright?"
- "Hey, don't criticize him, alright?"
- "Alright, alright, what's going on here?"

There are certain people who really do get upset when I use the word "alright" in the strip. And whenever I do it, they write to remind me that the correct term is "all right." So I thought I'd try and make their heads explode.

Panel 1:
- "GUARD DUCK HAS A NEW MISSION. HE'S GONNA SNEAK UP ON NEGATIVE PEOPLE AND BITE THEIR BUTTOCKS."
- "SOUNDS LAME."

Panel 2:
(Guard Duck leaping up from couch)

Panel 3:
- "LET'S TRY TO REMAIN POSITIVE."

I was going to make Guard Duck's living in the couch a regular thing, but I got bored with the concept after only three strips.

Panel 4:
- "IF YOUR COUCH DUCK IS GONNA TERRORIZE US BY HIDING IN THE CUSHIONS, WE NEED TO START STARVING HIM OUT."

Panel 5:
- "THERE'S ENOUGH FOOD IN HERE TO LAST THIRTY YEARS."

Panel 6:
- "WE SHOULD VACUUM UNDER THE CUSHIONS NOW AND THEN."

Panel 7:
- "OKAY, IF WE CAN'T STARVE OUT YOUR STUPID COUCH DUCK, WE CAN AT LEAST CLOSE HIS BANK ACCOUNTS. THAT WAY HE WON'T HAVE ANY CASH FOR NEW WEAPONS."

Panel 8:
- "THERE'S SEVENTY THOUSAND DOLLARS IN LOOSE CHANGE DOWN HERE."

Panel 9:
- "WE REALLY SHOULDA BEEN CHECKING UNDER THE CUSHIONS."

Given that I'm the father of two kids, I thought I'd try and give one of the characters a child. But none of my characters are really in relationships, so I had to just drop the kid off at his doorstep.

I really sort of regret this strip. It's just too trite. You can look at practically any family strip and see a joke about one of their kids playing too many video games. This was probably the first sign that I didn't know what to do with this new character.

A bit stuck for ideas, I thought I'd have him start tormenting the crocs.

Panel 1:
- Whuh we gonna do, Burt? Me keep geeting shot by blowdart assasseen. Buttocks een great pain.
- We is pray to God of crocs. He save us.

Panel 2:
- Hullo, God of Crocs. Dis Bob and Burt. Someone shoot us. Peese make stop now.

Panel 3:
- Dis why me atheist, Burt.

By this time, I've stopped showing the poor little zebra entirely.

Panel 4:
- Whuh you doing, Bob?
- Me geet new God, Burt. Yours no save us.

Panel 5:
- Yours juss box.
- He no juss box. He play moosic.

Panel 6: SPROING

Panel 7:
- Releegion very confusing, Bob.
- My God so vengeful!

Panel 8:
- YO, ZEEBS, WHAT HAPPENED TO YOUR SON, 'PLAID'?
- TURNS OUT HE WASN'T MY SON. I GUESS THERE ARE LOTS OF POTENTIAL ZEBRA DADS WITH STRIPES LIKE MINE, AND MY EX-GIRLFRIEND JUST PICKED THE WRONG ONE.

Panel 9:
- SOUNDS TO ME LIKE SOME WEASEL CARTOONIST DIDN'T KNOW WHERE TO GO WITH THE CHARACTER, SO HE JUST WIMPED OUT BY COMING UP WITH THAT STUPID EXPLANATION IN PANEL ONE.

Panel 10:
- THAT'S VERY INAPPROPRIATE.

Panel 11:
- THE WEASEL SPEAKS.
- HEY! YOU TRY COMING UP WITH 365 IDEAS A YEAR!!

I own up to my failings.

Panel 1:
— HEY, STEPHSTER, QUICK QUESTION.
— WHAT IS IT? I'M TRYING TO DRAW.

Panel 2:
— JUST CURIOUS... WHAT'S THE HIGHEST HONOR IN ALL OF CARTOONING?
— THE REUBEN AWARD. WHY?

Panel 3:
— THE REUBEN, HUH? I DON'T SUPPOSE YOU'VE EVER BEEN NOMINATED FOR THAT?
— WHERE IS THIS GOING?

Panel 4:
— NOWHERE. HEY, JUST WONDERING, YOU HAVEN'T BY CHANCE BEEN NOMINATED THREE YEARS IN A ROW, HAVE YOU?
— PLEASE... LEAVE.... RIGHT—

Panel 5:
— AND LOST MISERABLY EVERY SINGLE YEAR?!

Panel 6:
— I BUILT YOU A TROPHY SHELF. MIND IF I USE IT TO STORE GARBANZO BEANS?
— THE PANTRY IS SOOOOOO FULL.

The good news is that there is *still* plenty of space to store garbanzo beans, as I have now lost five years in a row. More importantly, look how well I drew that flying shoe. They should give me the Reuben for that shoe alone.

Panel 1 (strip 1):
- "LISTEN, STEPH, I KNOW THAT EVERY YEAR YOU'RE UP FOR CARTOONING'S HIGHEST AWARD, THE REUBEN, AND THAT EVERY YEAR YOU LOSE. SO NOW I FEEL BAD FOR BUILDING YOU THIS EMPTY TROPHY SHELF."
- "IS THAT SO?"

Panel 2:
- "YEAH, SO I BOUGHT YOU SOME DECORATIVE WOODEN LETTERS TO FILL THE SPACE. THEY'RE FUN TO REARRANGE IF YOU'RE EVER BORED."
- "WELL, I GUESS THAT'S PRETTY NICE OF YOU. THANKS."
- ROLES

Panel 3:
- "OH, LOOK. I'VE REARRANGED THEM."
- "TAKE THEM DOWN."
- "THAT DOES NOT LOOK LIKE A TROPHY."
- LOSER

Strip 2, Panel 1:
- "EXCUSE ME, SIR, BUT I JUST WANT TO SAY HOW SORRY I AM THAT RICHARD THOMPSON BEAT YOU FOR THE REUBEN AWARD LAST YEAR. THAT 'BEST CARTOONIST' TROPHY SHOULD REALLY BE YOURS."

Panel 2:
- "WHOA WHOA WHOA...THAT'S NOT TRUE. RICHARD DESERVED THAT TROPHY. HIS 'CUL DE SAC' STRIP IS AWESOME. PLUS, RICHARD IS A KINDHEARTED, SWEET, HUMBLE GUY."

Panel 3:
- "NOW I FEEL BAD FOR KNOCKING HIM UNCONSCIOUS."
- "TOLD YOU WE SHOULDN'T HAVE STOLEN THIS."

In 2012, I was fortunate enough to actually visit Richard Thompson's studio. I did not knock him unconscious.

Strip 3, Panel 1:
- "HEY, JEFF THE CYCLIST. WHAT ARE YOU HAVING FOR BREAKFAST TODAY?"
- "FIFTY GRAMS OF OATMEAL, ONE CUP OF BERRIES, AND A QUARTER CUP OF ALMONDS. IT'S ALL PART OF MY FITNESS REGIMEN."

Panel 2:
- "THAT'S GREAT. HAVING A FITNESS REGIMEN IS IMPORTANT."
- "ESSENTIAL. AND WHAT IS YOURS?"

Panel 3:
- "I'VE STOPPED FRYING MY TWINKIES."

No cyclist complained about this strip. I must be losing my touch.

Sometimes I look back at some of my strips and even *I* think they're dark. What's interesting is that they rarely correspond to depressed periods of my life. I tend to write these when I'm happy.

Hey, I got in a reference to both "hell" and winged ponies flying out of someone's @##. And if that doesn't win me the Reuben, I don't know what will.

PIGITA?
YES?
I HAVE SOMETHING TO CONFESS.
WHAT IS IT?
IT'S ABOUT US.
US??
I CHEATED ON YOU.
KSSSH
3/4
...BY LANDING ON 'MARVIN GARDENS' AND NOT PAYING YOU RENT.
OH.
YOU'RE A VERY INTENSE 'MONOPOLY' PLAYER.

Strip 1:

Panel 1: "WHAT'S WITH THE SIGN?" / "Me is support Newt Geengrich for Pressydent."

Panel 2: "WHAT FOR?" / "Newts is fellow reptile. WE IS DOMINATE WORLD!"

Panel 3: "NEWTS ARE AMPHIBIANS."

Panel 4: "Politics so disillusioning."

At the time these strips appeared, Newt Gingrich was still in the race to be the Republican nominee for president of the United States.

Strip 2:

Panel 1: "GEET OUT of way, family... Me campayning 'gainst Geengrich." / "SINCE WHEN DO YOU CARE ABOUT POLITICS?"

Panel 2: "Since amphibian try be Pressydent. Amphibians worst ting in world." / "LARRY, THAT NEWT IS A HUMAN."

Panel 3: "HAHAHAHAHA HAHAHAHAHA"

Panel 4: "And dat why we no let women vote, son." / "WOMEN CAN VOTE, DAD." / "LEMME SHOW YOU WHAT ELSE WOMEN CAN DO, LARRY."

Larry's line in the last panel really makes me laugh. I like how he thinks he's actually teaching Junior something.

Strip 3:

Panel 1: "WHY ARE YOU STILL CAMPAIGNING AGAINST NEWT GINGRICH, DAD?" / "Becuss amphibians beegest liars ever. One day dey has gills. One day dey has lungs. Dey like evil magicians."

Panel 2: "DAD...STOP...THIS NEWT'S A HUMAN. I BROUGHT A PHOTO OF HIM. SEE... WHAT DO YOU THINK?"

Panel 3: "Dat amphibians learn grow human head."

Panel 4: "NO." / "Guy probblee laying eggs een swamp right now."

166

I rarely try to actually draw a caricature of someone. You can see why.

As it turned out, neither of the panels was correct. Newt had neither won the nomination nor dropped out. His campaign was just sort of lingering, as it would until early May, when he finally dropped out.

167

The idea for this strip came from a reader who I believe was a criminal attorney. He told me that if I looked carefully at Blondie's hand, I would see that she was inadvertently flashing gang signs. I thought it was one of the funniest things I'd ever heard. So naturally, I did a strip about it. And sure enough, on the day this strip ran, Blondie flashed the sign again. It was perfect.

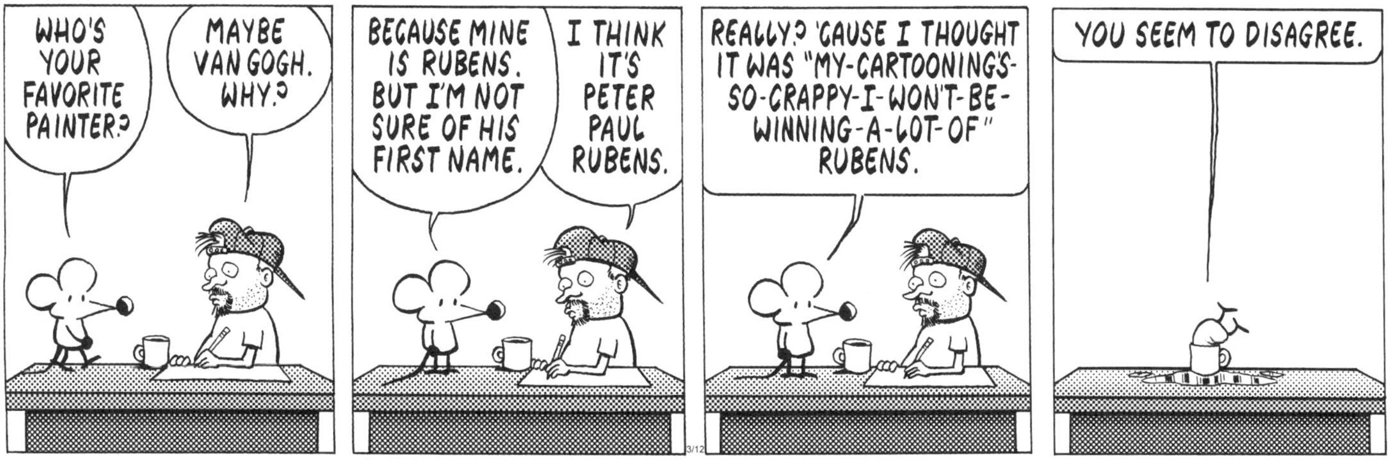
WHO'S YOUR FAVORITE PAINTER?
MAYBE VAN GOGH. WHY?
BECAUSE MINE IS RUBENS. BUT I'M NOT SURE OF HIS FIRST NAME.
I THINK IT'S PETER PAUL RUBENS.
REALLY? 'CAUSE I THOUGHT IT WAS "MY-CARTOONING'S-SO-CRAPPY-I-WON'T-BE-WINNING-A-LOT-OF" RUBENS.
YOU SEEM TO DISAGREE.

Here is all I know about the work of famed painter Peter Paul Rubens: He paints fat people.

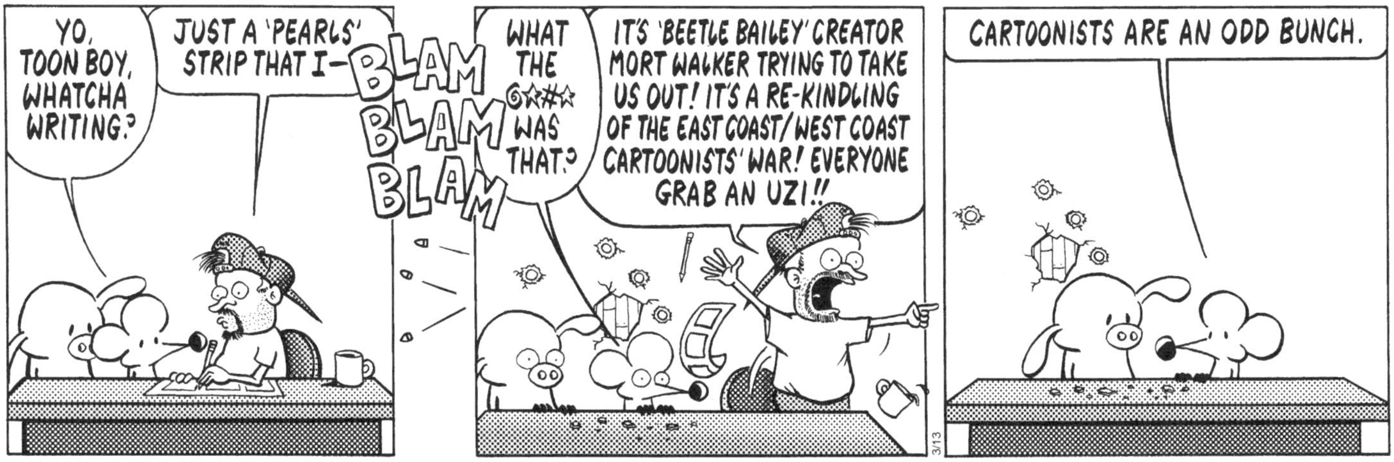
YO, TOON BOY, WHATCHA WRITING?
JUST A 'PEARLS' STRIP THAT I—
BLAM BLAM BLAM
WHAT THE @☆#☆ WAS THAT?
IT'S 'BEETLE BAILEY' CREATOR MORT WALKER TRYING TO TAKE US OUT! IT'S A RE-KINDLING OF THE EAST COAST/WEST COAST CARTOONISTS' WAR! EVERYONE GRAB AN UZI!!
CARTOONISTS ARE AN ODD BUNCH.

This was supposed to be my parody of the legendary East Coast/West Coast hip-hop wars of the 1990s. In this case, I based it on where the particular cartoonists lived. And since Mort Walker lives on the East Coast, and I live on the West, we were on opposite sides.

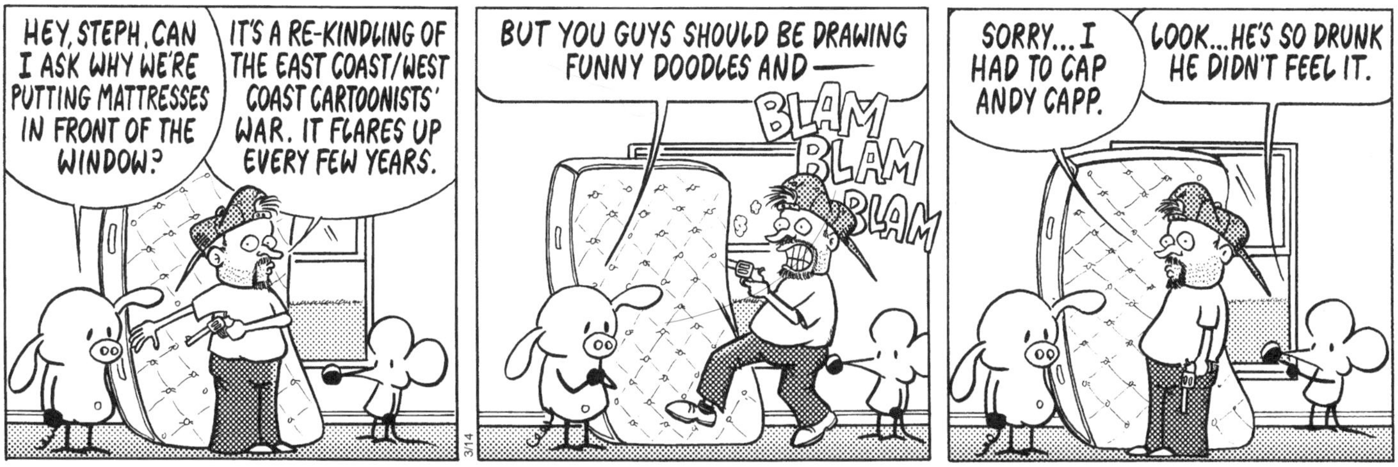
HEY, STEPH, CAN I ASK WHY WE'RE PUTTING MATTRESSES IN FRONT OF THE WINDOW?
IT'S A RE-KINDLING OF THE EAST COAST/WEST COAST CARTOONISTS' WAR. IT FLARES UP EVERY FEW YEARS.
BUT YOU GUYS SHOULD BE DRAWING FUNNY DOODLES AND—
BLAM BLAM BLAM
SORRY... I HAD TO CAP ANDY CAPP.
LOOK... HE'S SO DRUNK HE DIDN'T FEEL IT.

Three points here: 1) I do not like drawing mattresses; 2) People get very angry when I depict gun violence; and 3) I really like the line, "I had to cap Andy Capp."

Panel 1:
"LISTEN, PIG, THIS EAST COAST/WEST COAST CARTOONISTS' WAR IS GONNA GET UGLY, BUT DON'T WORRY, 'CAUSE WE HAVE THE ULTIMATE BAD@## ON OUR SIDE, AND THAT'S GUARD DUCK."

Panel 2:
"GEE, STEPH..I DUNNO..THE POOR GUY'S BEEN SO HIGH-STRUNG LATELY THAT I SENT HIM ON A RETREAT."
"RETREAT? TO WHERE?"

Panel 3:
"OHMMMMMMMMM"
TIBETAN PEACE, LOVE AND MEDITATION CENTER

Wow, I pretty clearly telegraphed the word "badass" here. So by this point in the week, I'm angering everybody.

Panel 4:
"STEPH, WHAT THE @#☆ IS THIS EAST COAST/WEST COAST CARTOONISTS' FEUD?"
ZING

Panel 5:
"SYNDICATION'S A ROUGH BUSINESS, GOAT, SO EVERY FEW YEARS, CARTOONISTS FROM THE EAST COAST FIGHT ALONGSIDE THEIR CHARACTERS AGAINST ALL OF US WEST COAST GUYS AND ALL OF OUR CHARACTERS."

Panel 6:
"BUT WE DON'T HAVE GUARD DUCK RIGHT NOW...WHAT WEST COAST CHARACTERS DO WE HAVE THAT CAN MAKE UP FOR THAT?"

Panel 7:
"SHOOT ME NOW."

Both the *Family Circus* and *Cathy* are on the West Coast's side because their creators Jeff Keane and Cathy Guisewite both live in California. And I know that because I have been to both of their houses and stolen silverware.

Panel 8:
THE CARTOONISTS' WAR
"RAT! RAT! THAT CUTE L'IL DOG AND CAT FROM 'MUTTS' BROKE IN AND KIDNAPPED STEPHAN AT KNIFEPOINT! THEY WANT $10,000 TO GIVE HIM BACK!"
"NEVER"

Panel 9:
"YOU DON'T WANT TO PAY?"
"I DON'T WANT STEPHAN BACK."

Panel 10:
"POOR STEPHAN."
"NOW IF THEY WANT CASH TO *KEEP* HIM, I'LL TALK."

170

Panel 1:
- WHAT ARE YOU DOING WITH A HAMMER?
- Ees genetic adaptation. Ees better equip us keel zeeba.

Panel 2:
- WHAT ARE YOU TALKING ABOUT?
- Bob here esspert. We hire heem essplain whole ting. He reely smart. Geev us superior knowledge.

Panel 3:
- YEAH, WELL, BOB'S INCORRECT. A GENETIC ADAPTATION TAKES PLACE OVER MILLIONS OF YEARS. PLUS, IT'S A MODIFICATION OF THE ANIMAL'S D.N.A., AND IT FUNDAMENTALLY CHANGES ITS INNATE ABILITY TO SURVIVE.

Panel 5:
- CRACK

Panel 6:
- Me fundamentally change Bob.

At the time I wrote this, I was reading Charles Darwin's *On the Origin of Species*, which truly, was quite boring. So I felt compelled to get *something* out of the book by making it the subject of a strip.

This strip and the next one just about pushed certain newspaper editors right over the edge. In fact, one paper in Canada refused to run them and insisted that we provide them with replacement strips. When asked why, the newspaper editor said, "The March 19 strip references torture and the March 20 strip has sexual content."

I knew this one would cause problems, particularly the "friends with benefits" line in the last panel. As one reader wrote to the *Winston-Salem Journal*, "I am very concerned as to how the writer of the cartoon *Pearls Before Swine* can take sweet, innocent characters from family-oriented cartoons and use them as the brunt of their brand of sick humor."

Strip 1 (3/22):

Panel 1: "SOMETIMES I WONDER IF I HAVE FAITH IN ANYTHING, BUT I'M NOT SURE I KNOW WHAT FAITH IS." "IT'S BELIEVING IN SOMETHING... TRUSTING AND RELYING ON IT WITHOUT QUESTION. IS THERE SOMETHING IN YOUR LIFE THAT MEETS THAT STANDARD?"

Panel 2: "CHEESE."

Panel 3: "MAYBE I DIDN'T DEFINE THAT WELL." "IF YOU'LL EXCUSE ME, I NEED TO BUILD A CHURCH."

Strip 2 (3/23):

Panel 1: "I GOT TWO HUNDRED COMPLAINTS ABOUT THIS FEBRUARY 8TH STRIP WHERE YOU SAY YOU TRY TO RUN OVER PEOPLE LIKE JEFF, THE ANNOYING CYCLIST." "BUT I'M JUST A CARTOON CHARACTER."

Panel 2: "THAT'S NOT HOW THESE PEOPLE VIEW IT. THEY SAY YOU'RE AN ADVOCATE... THAT YOU HAVE THE ABILITY TO AFFECT PEOPLE'S BEHAVIOR."

Panel 3: "BREAK STEPHAN'S FINGERS!! BREAK STEPHAN'S FINGERS!!"

Panel 4: "HAVING FUN?" "WHAT'S TAKING THESE PEOPLE SO LONG?"

I thought I'd have some fun with the outrage over the prior cycling strip. Apparently, March was "Anger the Masses Month."

Strip 3 (3/24):

Panel 1: "Dear Girls, I am not smart. I'm fat. I'm poor. And I'm ugly."

Panel 2: "Come and get me!"

Panel 3: "YOUR SINGLES AD LEAVES SOMETHING TO BE DESIRED."

And now I depict a homicide. Good thing the victim wasn't on a bike.

Panel 1:
- "WHERE'S RAT TODAY?"
- "SHOPPING. HE'S LOOKING FOR SOMETHING THAT LETS HIM SIT WHEREVER HE WANTS YET ALWAYS HAVE A BEER HANDY."

Panel 2:
SQUEAK SQUEAK SQUEAK SQUEAK SQUEAK

Panel 3:
"GOTTA LOVE THE BABY STORE."

You have to admit, it'd be convenient.

Panel 4:
- "I CAN'T BELIEVE IT. YOU'RE REALLY GOING TO GO AROUND IN A BABY WALKER?"
- "YUP. I JUST ROLL AROUND AND DRINK BEER. MY GOAL IS TO NEVER HAVE TO GET UP TO DO ANYTHING AGAIN."

Panel 5:
"WELL, YOU'LL OBVIOUSLY HAVE TO GET UP TO DO SOME THINGS."

Panel 6:
- "I GOT WHAT YOU ASKED ME TO GET, RAT."
- "I'M GOING NOW."
- "NO, NO. *I'M* GOING NOW."

Can't believe I got away with this. Clearly, my editors are more lax than they used to be.

Panel 7:
- "HOW'S IT GOING, SIR?"
- "NOT GOOD, L'IL GUARD DUCK. I'M HAVING FRIENDS OVER FOR LUNCH AND I CAN'T GET THE MAYONNAISE LID LOOSE."

Panel 8:
BLAM!!

Panel 9:
- "IT'S LOOSE NOW, SIR."
- "WELL, NOW, THAT'S A HANDY-DANDY KITCHEN DEVICE."

Panel 1 (3/29):
- "IF THE CHOICE WAS YOURS, HOW WOULD YOU CHOOSE TO DIE?"
- "I DON'T KNOW... I GUESS RIGHT HERE DRAWING AT MY DRAWING TABLE."
- "BY NATURAL CAUSES."
- "FELT PRETTY NATURAL TO ME."

I recently went to Louisville, where they have a whole museum dedicated to the Louisville Slugger bat. I expected free admission given how often Rat uses their fine product, but I didn't get it.

Panel 2 (3/30):
- "HEY, NEIGHBOR MELANIE! HOW ARE THINGS? HOW'S YOUR HUSBAND?"
- "TERRIFIC, PIG! WE'VE BEEN GETTING ALONG GREAT EVER SINCE WE DECIDED TO COMMUNICATE BETTER AND BE MORE OPEN WITH EACH OTHER."
- "WHAT ARE YOU TWO YAPPING ABOUT?"
- "OH, SORRY, RAT. THIS IS MELANIE. SHE AND HER HUSBAND NOW HAVE AN OPEN MARRIAGE."
- "WELL, NOW. HER MOOD SURE CHANGED FAST."

My characters have surprisingly malleable skulls.

Panel 3 (3/31):
- "WHAT DO YOU DREAM OF BEING WHEN YOU'RE OLDER?"
- "OH, A TOY SHOP OWNER! I'D HAVE ALL THE TOYS I EVER WANTED FOR *FREE!!*"
- "TOY SHOP OWNERS DON'T GET TOYS FOR FREE. THEY PAY FOR THEM."
- "LIFE IS CRUEL."

Unlike most of my drawings, I really like the way this one came out. Especially the chest bump.

Read this with those special 3D glasses on and let me know if it looks any better.

This strip was the subject of a special caption contest run by Chronicle Books, the publisher of the *Pearls* iPad app, *Only the Pearls*. The idea was for readers to send in their own punch line. But I didn't really like any of them, so I just wrote one myself.

Panel 1:
- "What are you doing, Rat?"
- "Studying how to be a knight from the Middle Ages. These guys hated talking to the idiots around them so much that they hid inside a suit of metal."

Panel 2:
- "What are you talking about? That's not why knights wore armor. They wore it because—"

Panel 4:
- "That's rather rude."
- "Nuts. I can still hear ye."

I draw an awesome suit of armor. That's good to know, because if I ever lose this *Pearls* gig, I could always get a job drawing *Prince Valiant*.

Panel 1:
- "Where's Rat today?"
- "He has to spend Easter with his family."

Panel 2:
- "I thought he hated spending holidays with his family."
- "He does, but he says he has a way of dealing with it now."

Panel 3:
- "We know you're in there."

And I draw an awesome sliced ham. Wonder if there are any comic strips starring sliced ham?

Panel 1:
- "Why do people hate each other over racial and religious and political differences when it's so obvious that fundamentally there are only two kinds of people?"
- "Which are what?"

Panel 2:
- "Good people and people who use the word 'whom'."

Panel 3:
- "To whom are you referring?"
- "Whomer, repent!"
- Sign: "LOVE THE WHO, HATE THE WHOMER"

I've never liked whomers.

Panel 1:
- WHAT DO YOU HAVE THERE, PIG?
- SOME OF MY PEZ COLLECTION.

Panel 2:
- I DIDN'T KNOW YOU COLLECTED PEZ.
- OH, YEAH. IT'S GREAT TRYING TO COLLECT THE BEST ONES.

Panel 3:
- WHAT DO YOU LOOK FOR?
- THE ONES WITH THE MOST 'PEZNESS.'

Panel 4:
- WHAT'S THAT?
- PROPER HEAD-TO-BODY RATIO, COLOR, AND MOST OF ALL, RARITY.

Panel 5:
- AND WHICH ONES HAVE ALL THAT?
- PEZNESS? GOSH, WELL, MY YODA, THE TIN MAN, MY WILLIAM SHATNER. BUT THE BEST OF THE BEST IS THE ONE OF THE STAND-UP COMIC MARGARET CHO. ALMOST NO ONE HAS IT.

Panel 6:
- THAT ONE'S GOOD?
- GOOD?

Panel 7:
- THERE'S NOOOO PEZNESS LIKE CHO PEZNESS!

Panel 8:
- I MADE IT USING HIS ACTUAL HEAD.

Margaret Cho never contacted me in response to this strip. Neither did Yoda or the Tin Man.

I take back what I said earlier about me drawing an awesome suit of armor. This one is pretty bad. There goes my gig at *Prince Valiant*.

This is not my favorite croc series. Something's just off. I shall close my eyes during the next few strips.

UPDATE: Bob and Larry have set up a "Godfather"-inspired hit on Zebra at a restaurant. But no gun was waiting for Bob in the bathroom. Instead, his only available weapon is toilet paper.

How me 'spose hit zeeba wid toilet paper?

Zeeba have thin skull. Toilet paper bust right throo.

Eef you say so. But me gonna grab rest of package just een case it... ...UH OH.

Whuh? Whuh?

Ees Esstra Soft.

ABORT! ABORT!

I'm not looking. I'm not looking.

STORY UPDATE Unable to pull off the "Godfather"-style hit on Zebra with extra-soft toilet paper, the crocs send Bob out for a better weapon... regular toilet paper.

Me not want do dis, Larry. Ees humiliating buy T.P.

Shut face, Bob. Peoples buy T.P. all time.

HEY, YOU KNOW, THERE'S A TWO-FOR-ONE SALE ON THAT... LET ME JUST GET SOMEONE TO —
NO NO NO NO NO NO
CAN I GET ONE PACK OF REGULAR TOILET PAPER FOR A CUSTOMER ON AISLE TWO WHOSE BACKSIDE MUST NOT BE EXTRA-SENSITIVE?

YOU MISTER HARD-BUTT?

Me not know nutting.

PLEASE TAKE YOUR TOILET PAPER, CAPTAIN STONE CHEEKS!

Okay, this one is slightly redeemed by the "Captain Stone Cheeks" line. I like that.

STORY UPDATE Larry and Bob have bought the hardest toilet paper they can find to bash Zebra over the head while he is on a date at a restaurant.

Okay, Larry, me behind Zeeba booth holding seecret weapon.

Okay. Time bash Zeeba's soft skull. End years o' croc misery. God bless you face. KEEL.

We got techneekal deeficulties, Larry.

182

| Danny Donkey hated people. "It's true." | So Danny Donkey bought a treehouse at the top of a very tall tree. | "You should invite the entire neighborhood to a housewarming party," said Danny's perky real estate agent. "Then you'll have good relationships with all your neighbors." |

| So Danny Donkey invited all his neighbors to a housewarming party. | Which went well until he ran out of champagne. "You ran out of champagne, dude." "Yeah. You call this a party?" | So Danny excused himself to buy more champagne. "More bubbly on the way." | And chopped down the tree. "Ahhh" "No" "Scream" "Timb-e-e-e-r" |

| "Now I have good relationships with all my neighbors," exclaimed Danny Donkey. | 'So remember, kids, it's not good fences that make good neighbors. It's deceased neighbors that make good neighbors.' "I give up." "Are all these people with X's for eyes just napping?" |

This one got complaints, which really surprised me. What angered people was the fact that Danny became happy by killing all his neighbors. I guess I never looked at it that way. I just thought it was funny that Danny would excuse himself to buy more champagne and then chop down the tree. So what does this teach us? That either people are too uptight or I'm sociopathic.

Strip 1:

- WHAT ARE YOU DOING, PIG?
- JUST GETTING OUTSIDE FOR A CHANGE...ENJOYING NATURE...IT'S SO PEACEFUL...SO HARMONIOUS...THE BIRDS, THE FISH, THE INSECTS...
- ALL OF WHOM ARE TRYING TO KILL EACH OTHER.
- LET'S NEVER LEAVE THE LIVING ROOM AGAIN.

Look at those realistically rendered birch trees in the background. It's almost like you're looking at a photograph.

Strip 2:

- WITH ALL THESE NEW TECHNOLOGIES COMING OUT EVERY DAY, DOESN'T IT SOMETIMES FEEL LIKE WE'RE LIVING IN AN AGE OF MIRACLES?
- OH, YEAH. LIKE HOW WHEN YOU PULL OUT A KLEENEX, THE NEXT ONE MIRACULOUSLY APPEARS?
- NO.
- HOW DO THEY *DO IT*?

Strip 3:

- HEY, GOAT, SORRY THAT YESTERDAY I WAS SO AMAZED AT HOW WHEN YOU PULL A KLEENEX OUT OF THE BOX, THE NEXT ONE AUTOMATICALLY APPEARS. RAT EXPLAINED TO ME HOW THEY DO IT.
- THAT'S OKAY, PIG... AT LEAST NOW YOU UNDERSTAND.
- YEAH. BUT HOW DO THEY GET THAT LITTLE MAN IN THERE WHO RADIOS BACK TO KLEENEX HEADQUARTERS?
- HE'S VERY SMALL.
- DO YOU NEED FOOD?!
- CHECK, PLEASE.

Think of how much more Kleenex you'd buy if there really was a tiny man in the box. Then again, it would probably break a few labor laws.

Strip 1 (4/19):

Pig: WHAT ARE YOU DOING, PIG?

Rat: TRYING TO FIND KLEENEX BOB. HE'S THE LITTLE MAN IN THE KLEENEX BOX WHO RADIOS BACK TO HEADQUARTERS WHENEVER YOU TAKE OUT A KLEENEX.

Pig: WHAT ARE YOU TALKING ABOUT?

Rat: IT'S HOW KLEENEX HEADQUARTERS KNOWS TO POP THE NEXT KLEENEX OUT OF THE BOX! HE'S A CRITICAL PART OF THE OPERATION! AND I CAN'T FIND HIM ANYWHERE! BECAUSE HE'S LOST! LOST!

Rat: I THINK I'LL SHOW MYSELF OUT.

Pig: SHHH. SENDING IN A SEARCH PARTY.

Strip 2 (4/20):

Goat: HEY, RAT.... HOW COME PIG WASN'T AT THE DINER THIS MORNING?

Rat: HE HAS GOOSEBUMPS.

Goat: SINCE WHEN DO GOOSEBUMPS KEEP SOMEONE FROM GOING OUT FOR COFFEE?

Goose (with bat): NEXT TIME PAY YOUR DEBTS.

Goat: NEVER MIND.

Rat: LOOK...IT'S A GOOSEKICKTOTHE-GROIN.

Yet another endorsement of Louisville Slugger. My, those people owe me.

Strip 3 (4/21):

Rat: LOOK AT ALL THIS E-MAIL. I'VE GOT HUNDREDS I HAVEN'T EVEN READ.

Pig: HOW DO YOU RESPOND TO ALL THOSE?

Rat: WELL, ONE LITTLE SHORTCUT I'VE LEARNED IS TO FIRST CLICK THE 'SELECT ALL' FEATURE.

Pig: THEN WHAT?

[Delete]

Rat: IT'S A BIG TIME-SAVER.

I've found that yelling, "I'm Stephan Pastis, darn it," really is not an effective means of getting what I want from someone. Though yelling, "I'm Bill Watterson, darn it," has worked once or twice.

Panel 1:
- "I HATE EVERYBODY. I HATE EVERYTHING."
- "YOU KNOW, IF YOU'RE SO UNHAPPY, YOU SHOULD THINK ABOUT MOVING ABROAD."

Panel 2: (no dialogue)

Panel 3: "DIDN'T HELP."

This is one of my favorite strips of the year. It half makes up for that lousy croc-in-the-bathroom series.

Panel 1:
- "Hullo zeeba neighba. Leesten. You got long arms? Me drop keys through grate."
- "OH, YOU MEAN THE SEWER GRATE?"

Panel 2: "Barbeecue."

Panel 3: "Dat guy never helpful."

Panel 1:
- "I JUST READ THOMAS MANN'S NOVEL 'DEATH IN VENICE.'"
- "GREAT. THAT'S A REAL CLASSIC."

Panel 2: "OH, AND I CAN SEE WHY. MAN GOES TO VENICE. MAN DIES."

Panel 3: "A CLASSIC!!!"

Panel 4:
- "MAYBE GREAT LITERATURE ISN'T YOUR THING."
- "SO IS 'CLASSIC' CODE FOR BORING AND SUCKY?"

I really did read this book. If you are tempted to waste your time on it, do something more productive instead, like digging a hole in your backyard and then filling it back up.

HEY, RAT... I'D LIKE YOU TO MEET OUR NEWEST CHARACTER, MIKEY THE MOLE.

THAT'S IT?... HE'S JUST A MOLE? NO WEIRD FREAKISH TRAIT LIKE ALL OUR OTHER CHARACTERS?

FOOSHHH

HE DOES SPONTANEOUSLY COMBUST.

IT'S ALWAYS SOMETHING.

FEEL FREE TO ROAST MARSH-MALLOWS.

Mikey the Spontaneously Combusting Mole would make a dangerous kids toy.

HEY, RAT, I COULDN'T HELP BUT NOTICE YOU'RE NOT EATING YOUR SOUP THE RIGHT WAY.... WHEN YOU DIP THE SPOON, YOU'RE SUPPOSED TO MOVE IT AWAY FROM YOU, NOT TOWARD YOU.

LIKE THAT?

JAB JAB JAB

NOT QUITE.

SHOULD I TRY AGAIN, MISS MANNERS?

I think my mom really did try to teach me this one time. Though I did not poke her in the eye.

WHAT ARE YOU DOING, PIG?

PLAYING PING PONG WITH RAT.

BUT HE'S JUST SMASHING THE BALL INTO YOUR FACE.

YEAH. RAT SAYS THE 'PING' IS WHEN YOU HIT IT WITH THE PADDLE, BUT THE 'PONG' IS WHEN YOU SMASH SOMEONE'S FACE. OTHERWISE, HE SAYS IT'D BE CALLED 'PING PING.'

THAT IS NOT HOW YOU PLAY—

MAY I ONE DAY BE A PINGER?

A PONGER BE A PINGER? NOW I HAVE TO PADDLE YOU FOR ASKING.

Hullooo, zeeba neighba, leesten... Crocs buy eendustrial strengf trash compakker.

WHAT FOR?

Shove you eenside. Crush you like Hefty bag.

DO YOU THINK THAT CAN CRUSH AN ANIMAL MY SIZE?

Do me tink? Me know. Me and Burt be like professional scientist. Did many test.

WHERE'S BURT?

He scream a lot for professional scientist.

The way you know that's a trash compactor and not a dishwasher is that I refer to it as a trash compactor. Well, "trash compakker."

Panel 1 (strip 1):
- "DID YOU HEAR THAT THE GRIM REAPER GUY IS MOVING BACK INTO THE HOUSE NEXT DOOR TO YOU? I GUESS HE AND MRS. DEATH WERE SEPARATED FOR A WHILE."
- "YEAH, I SURE MISSED MR. DEATH. I'M EVEN MAKING A SIGN ON BEHALF OF THE NEIGHBORHOOD WELCOMING HIM BACK."

Panel 2: Sign reads "THIS TOWN WELCOMES DEATH"

Panel 3:
- "MAYBE WE COULD RE-WORD THAT."
- "HOW 'BOUT THIS?"
- Sign: "EAGERLY AWAITING DEATH"

I occasionally get requests to bring back Pig's Grim Reaper neighbor. So I listened and brought him back. I'm a very consumer-friendly cartoonist.

Strip 2, Panel 1:
- "HEY THERE, PIG. JUST WANTED TO SAY THANKS FOR BEING SO NICE AND WELCOMING ME BACK TO THE NEIGHBORHOOD."
- "IT'S MY PLEASURE, MR. DEATH. HEY, HOW COME YOU'RE NOT WEARING THE GIFT I GOT YOU? I BOUGHT IT ON MY LAST VACATION."

Panel 2:
- "OH, THAT?... WELL... I..."
- "OH, C'MON, MR. DEATH. YOU'RE REALLY GONNA HURT MY FEELINGS."

Panel 3:
- "HAPPY?"
- "YOU LOOK SOOOO CUTE."

I have not yet been sued by Disney.

Strip 3, Panel 1:
- "LOOK AT THAT GUY HOLDING HIS CELL PHONE SO CLOSE TO HIS HEAD. DO YOU THINK IT'S TRUE THAT THOSE THINGS CAN BE DANGEROUS TO YOUR HEALTH?"
- "YAP YAP YAP YAP YAP YAP YAP YAP YAP"

Panel 2: CRACK

Panel 3: "SOMETIMES."

Panel 1:
- HEY, PIG, I WANT YOU TO MEET ONE OF THE BEST ENTERTAINMENT LAWYERS IN HOLLYWOOD..... I'M SELLING A 'PEARLS' MOVIE SCRIPT AND HE'S GONNA HELP ME.
- HI. I'M LES ABELL.

Panel 2:
- OHH, DON'T SAY THAT. I BET IF YOU TRY A LITTLE HARDER, ONE DAY YOU'LL BE JUST AS GOOD AS ALL THE OTHER LAWYERS.

Panel 3:
- WHAT THE G*#@ IS HE TALKING ABOUT?
- PIG... HE'S LES ABELL.
- WELL, DON'T SAY IT IN FRONT OF HIM.

That really was the name of my attorney, although we never did sell the script.

Panel 1:
- 'PROMOTE PEACE'....'CO-EXIST.'... 'SAVE THE PLANET.'... WHY DO PEOPLE ALWAYS TELL ME WHAT TO DO ON THEIR BUMPER STICKERS?
- I DON'T KNOW. WHY DOES IT MATTER?

Panel 2:
- BECAUSE IT BOTHERS ME. SO I'VE CREATED MY OWN.

Panel 3:
- Stop telling me what to do on your bumper stickers.

Panel 4:
- I THINK IT HURTS YOUR CASE THAT IT'S ON A BUMPER STICKER.
- HEY. STOP TELLING ME WHAT TO DO.

Panel 1:
- WHAT'S THE KEY TO BEING HAPPY?
- I THINK IT'S LEARNING TO LIVE IN THE MOMENT.

Panel 2:
- WHICH MOMENT? BECAUSE MANY OF MINE ARE CRAPPY.

Panel 3:
- THIS MOMENT.
- THIS MOMENT? OH, HOW BORING.

More and more, I am finding that I can get away with words like "crap" and "crappy." I guess I have finally broken the will of editors nationwide.

This was the most popular *Pearls* strip of the year. I guess a lot of people related to it.

Panel 1:
- Pig: WELL, GOAT, I'M OFF... I JOINED 'TOASTMASTERS INTERNATIONAL' AND HAVE MY FIRST MEETING.
- Goat: GOOD FOR YOU, PIG. ARE YOU GOING TO IMPROVE YOUR PUBLIC SPEAKING SKILLS?

Panel 3:
- IT APPEARS THERE'S BEEN A MISUNDERSTANDING.

I got requests from Toastmasters International for permission to use this strip in various newsletters and on web sites. Perhaps they have a number of confused members who bring toasters to meetings.

Panel 1:
- Goat: WHAT'S THE MATTER WITH YOU, PIG?
- Pig: IT'S MY NEIGHBOR, JUAN. HE'S SO RUDE TO PEOPLE, BUT I DON'T THINK HE REALIZES IT.

Panel 2:
- Goat: WELL, IT CAN BE PAINFUL FOR SOME PEOPLE TO SEE THEMSELVES AS THEY TRULY ARE.
- Pig: SO IT ACHES JUAN TO KNOW JUAN?

Panel 3:
- SURELY, YOU CAN DO BETTER.

Panel 1:
- Pig: HEY, PIGITA... MY NEIGHBORS BOB AND BETTY ASKED IF WE'D BE INTERESTED IN DOING SOMETHING WITH THEM.

Panel 2:
- Pigita: I DON'T KNOW ANYTHING ABOUT THEM.
- Pig: WELL, FOR ONE THING, THEY'RE SWINGERS.

Panel 3:
- SHE DOESN'T APPROVE OF YOUR LIFESTYLE.

Easy joke, but it still made me laugh.

My cousin Louis really does own a cheese shop. It's in South Pasadena, California. Stop by and tell him I sent you. Then ask him for free cheese. He won't give it to you, but it will annoy him, and that amuses me.

Shortly before this ran, *Doonesbury* creator Garry Trudeau published a series of strips dealing with abortion restrictions in Texas, and I guess it upset a few newspaper editors. Sensitive to that, my syndicate called me and told me I could not run this strip. That really surprised me, as I had not had a strip rejected by my syndicate in many years, and I didn't think this particular strip was that offensive. So I argued with my syndicate, and after a series of phone calls back and forth, they finally allowed me to run it. And as it turned out, it generated very few complaints, proving once again that I am always, always right.

194

Panel 1:
— BOB! BOB! Guess whuh me see.
— Whuh?

Panel 2:
— Dead deer. On highway. Stoopid tings try run across. Geet hit.
— Dead deer taste gud.

Panel 3:
— Me know dat, Bob. So go steal beegest truck possible. We zoom down highway. Run over everyting.

Panel 4:
(wordless — Bob runs off, hat and beer can flying)

Panel 5:
(croc standing by golf cart with other croc driving it)

Panel 6:
— How 'bout YOU go run across highway, Bob?
— GIMME BACK THE CART, PAL.
— Peese no hit me, Man-Een-Funny-Pants.

Given how long it took me to draw that golf cart, I can tell you with a fair degree of certainty that you will never see another golf cart in *Pearls*.

I don't know very much about flamethrowers, but I'm guessing it's not proper protocol to use one while smoking a cigarette.

This arose from an interview with a comedian that I heard on NPR's *Fresh Air*. It just got so tiresome to hear the guy talk about all his problems. Thus, I mocked him.

Mister Muffatoni reminds me of an older *Pearls* character, Pepito the Sock Puppet. I guess I find violent puppets entertaining.

I just know that someone out there has now tried to make this ringtone.

No Amish complained.

I knew people weren't going to like the idea of somebody shooting a horse, so I made him 1) arrogant; and 2) French, and that seemed to make everything okay.

For those of you wondering, that's a flame in the third panel. It is not a prickly bush.

We pretty much always buy the cheapest gift on anyone's wedding registry. And that means towels. Lots and lots of towels.

Holy smokes, did this one create confusion. Newspaper readers everywhere thought *Pearls* had been cancelled and replaced by the comic strip *Zits*. As one reader wrote, "I panicked, ripped (the comics section) in half, and threw it away."

Panel 1:
MY STUPID KNOW-IT-ALL COUSIN FROM NEW ORLEANS WANTS TO VISIT ME... HE'S THAT GUY WHO EVEN WHEN HE ASKS A QUESTION JUST DOES IT SO HE CAN SHOW YOU WHAT HE KNOWS.

Panel 2:
ISN'T HE THAT ONE FROM THE GARDEN DISTRICT WHERE ALL THE WEALTHY TOBACCO, COTTON AND SUGAR MERCHANTS BUILT THEIR HOMES ALONG ST. CHARLES AVENUE IN THE 1840s AND '50s WHEN NEW ORLEANS WAS THE SECOND BIGGEST PORT IN THE UNITED STATES?

Panel 3:
ISN'T SUGAR THE THING I'M ABOUT TO JAM UP YOUR NOSE?
CHECK PLEASE.
YES! YES! THAT *IS* SUGAR!

"Check please" is a pretty trite line. But I know it's trite. And that makes it okay.

Panel 1:
HEY, DAD, I KNOW YOU THINK AMPHIBIANS ARE SHIFTY AND UNTRUSTWORTHY, BUT I WANT YOU TO KNOW I'VE BECOME FRIENDS WITH ONE. HE'S FREDDY THE FROG, AND I'D LIKE YOU TO TREAT HIM WITH RESPECT.

Panel 2:
SHAKE SHAKE SHAKE SHAKE SHAKE

Panel 3:
Just making sure he no steal silverware.

Panel 1:
So, amphibian... You is start life wid tail, live underwater. Den one day—POOF—you lose tail, live on land... How you essplain?
I DUNNO. I GUESS JUST EVOLUTION. HOW WOULD YOU EXPLAIN IT?

Panel 2:
Mebbe you worship Satan?

Panel 3:
OKAY, DAD, TIME TO GO.
Show us you horns, leetle devil frog.

If you haven't noticed, I only know how to draw an empty beer can one way. And that is from a side view facing to the left. Perhaps if I continue drawing *Pearls* for another twelve years, I will learn how to draw one facing to the right.

For those of you who think *Pearls* is dark, read the ending of *Of Mice and Men*, a book that is required reading for many high school students. It makes *Pearls* look positively uplifting.

"Ja" means "yes" in German. And this has been your educational moment for the day.

Elly Elephant sat alone staring at the sugar dispenser. "OH, THAT I COULD MEET SOMEONE TO SHARE MY LIFE."	And poof, the Marriage Fairy appeared. "TELL ME YOUR WISH. AND IT SHALL BE YOURS."	But before Elly could answer, she ran into her friend, Rita Rabbit. "WHAT'S WRONG, RITA RABBIT?"
"My husband was supposed to meet me here," she said, "but he's an hour late."	"He's always an hour late. Always. Doesn't call. Nothing. That is, when he even remembers me."	"Of course, if it's his friends, it's different," said Rita Rabbit. "Then he drops everything."

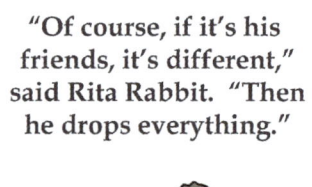

"It's just so frustrating, Elly Elephant. To be married, but so alone. What would you do if you were me?"

Elly Elephant crushed the Marriage Fairy with the sugar dispenser. **WHAM**

"WELL NOW, THAT'S A HEARTWARMING TALE." "'NOW SMASH HER WITH THE SALT SHAKER!' YELLED RITA RABBIT." "RUN FROM THE CONDIMENTS, L'IL FAIRY!!"

If you read through the entire sixty-four-year history of *Beetle Bailey*, I bet you will never see the line, "Run from the condiments, L'il Fairy!" And that is why I am the groundbreaking cartoonist that I am.

204

Panel 1:
- HI, JUNIOR. WHAT ARE YOU WATCHING?
- FREDDY THE FROG. HE AND HIS FAMILY ARE MOVING IN ACROSS THE STREET.

Panel 2:
- REALLY?... I DON'T THINK WE'VE HAD AMPHIBIANS ON THE BLOCK BEFORE.
- I KNOW, MOM. WHICH IS WHY WE NEED TO DO EVERYTHING WE CAN TO MAKE THEM FEEL AS WELCOME AS POSSIBLE.

Panel 3:
- BOOOOOOOO.

Panel 4:
- MAKE DAD GO INSIDE.
- WHERE YOU TAIL, FORMER FISH?

My best (and only) friend, Emilio, has a habit of booing everyday things. A bartender gives him the wrong drink. He boos. A person cuts in front of him in line. He boos. It makes me laugh every time.

Panel 1:
- LISTEN, DAD, YOU NEED TO ADJUST TO THE FACT THAT WE'RE GONNA HAVE AMPHIBIANS LIKE FREDDY LIVING ACROSS THE STREET.
- OKAY. ME LEARN ADJUST.
- THANKS, MR. LARRY.

Panel 3:
- PUTTING ON BLINDERS IS NOT ADJUSTING TO FREDDY.
- FREDDY? WHO DIS FREDDY?
- OVER HERE, MR. LARRY.

Panel 1:
- WHAT DO YOU HAVE THERE, RAT?
- A PERSON. I GOT HIM AT THE PERSON STORE.

Panel 2:
- IS HE HARD TO CARE FOR?
- NOT REALLY. YOU JUST GIVE HIM A FLATSCREEN AND ESPN AND HE'LL SIT THERE FOR HOURS.

Panel 3:
- WANT TO GIVE HIM A TREAT?

I regret not doing more of these "person pet" strips. Maybe I'll bring the character back.

Random trivia: Believe it or not, the first toilet flush ever heard on television was not until 1971 when the character Archie Bunker flushed the toilet on an episode of *All in the Family*. Apparently, people did not go to the bathroom in the 1950s and '60s.

One time I found some *Pearls Before Swine* books for sale at a car wash in Santa Rosa, California. That's not particularly interesting, but when you have to fill a whole book with commentary, you sometimes have to stretch.

Panel 1:
- Hey there, Pig...you look happy.
- I am! I just measured myself. I'm five feet, nine inches tall!

Panel 2:
- Gee, Pig...that sounds a little high.
- Well, I did measure myself with shoes.

Panel 3:
- Even with shoes, that sounds high.
- Here, measure for yourself. I'll stand against that fence.

Panel 5:
- I think I see the problem.
- You misjudged? It's okay. We all make mental booboos.

Is it just me, or do my characters look like they're walking on the back of a dead giraffe?

Panel row 1:

"Hey, son... Where my wife? Me want her sign petition against sheefty amphibian thieves moving eento neighbahood."

"She's at the hairdresser, Dad... and Freddy's family are not thieves... they're—"

"AH!" "HE STEAL WIFE HAIR!"

"Excuse us, Junior. I'd like to talk to your dad." "Why you blame me? He one make you look terrible."

Changing Patty's hair was a big mistake, because I could never remember if it was supposed to be black or orange. So in succeeding Sunday strips, you'll see it occasionally changes color.

Panel row 2:

"Hey, Rat, I'm home!" "Where you been?"

"Grocery store... Did you know they have sprayers now that go off in the produce section?" "Yeah. They're for keeping the produce from wilting."

"That's what they're for?" "Yeah. Why?"

"No reason."

Panel row 3:

"I hear you're upset about your new frog neighbors." "Yeah. Me hate slimy amphibians almost as much me hate you."

"Well, the reason that they're 'slimy' is that they breathe through their skin. If their skin isn't moist, they can't do that."

"Why are you blow-drying Freddy?" "Ohh, juss styling hair."

Another fallen beer can facing left. Because that is the only way beer cans fall.

Panel 1:
- Goat: GOSH, THAT WOMAN SITTING NEXT TO ME SURE IS PRETTY.
- Rat: WELL, SAY SOMETHING TO HER. NOTHING'S GONNA HAPPEN IF YOU JUST SIT THERE.

Panel 2:
- Goat: EXCUSE ME, BUT DID YOU KNOW THAT THE CHILDREN'S SONG, 'RING AROUND THE ROSIE, A POCKETFUL OF POSIES, ASHES, ASHES, WE ALL FALL DOWN,' IS ACTUALLY A REFERENCE TO THE BLACK DEATH, A PLAGUE THAT KILLED MILLIONS?

Panel 3:
- Goat: PERHAPS SILENCE IS THE BETTER APPROACH.

What Goat says in the second panel is actually not true. Which is why you should never cite *Pearls* in your doctoral dissertation.

Panel 1:
- Goat: DO YOU HAVE ANY ASPIRATIONS IN LIFE?
- Rat: I AM A REALIST. AND AS A REALIST, I MOCK THE LOFTY ASPIRATIONS OF OTHERS AND MAINTAIN FOR MYSELF BUT ONE SIMPLE GOAL.

Panel 2:
- Goat: WHICH IS WHAT?
- Rat: TO BE SO GREAT THAT WHEN I DIE, THE WORLD ENDS.

Panel 3:
- Goat: TRY HUMILITY.
- Rat: IN THE RACE FOR GREATNESS, HUMILITY IS BUT A BOOBY PRIZE.

I really like Rat's line in the last panel. Please take the time to submit it to *Bartlett's Book of Quotations* so that one day I can be remembered as great. So great that when I die, the world ends.

Panel 1:
- Rat: WHAT'S THIS COUCH DOING OUT HERE ON THE CURB?
- Pig: IT'S NEIGHBOR BOB'S. IT'S HOW HE GETS RID OF STUFF HE DOESN'T WANT. A LOT OF PEOPLE DO IT.

Panel 2:
- Rat: IT'S JUST THAT EASY?
- Pig: YUP.

Panel 3:
- Pig: SOME THINGS I JUST SHOULDN'T MENTION.

Panel 1:
- "HEY, RAT, I'D LIKE YOU TO MEET MY FRIEND, HANNAH HIPPO."
- "HEY."
- "WELL, HELLO... I'D LOVE TO CHAT MORE, BUT I SIMPLY *MUST* BE LEAVING."

Panel 3:
- "DIDN'T SHE SAY SHE WAS LEAVING?"
- "OH, THAT'S JUST HANNAH'S WAY. SHE'S THE HIPPO WHO SAYS GOODBYE, BUT NEVER LEAVES."

Panel 4:
- "I HATE THAT... WHEN YOU SAY GOODBYE, GET OUT. DON'T LINGER. LEAVE. YOUR CHAT PRIVILEGES ARE REVOKED."
- "I HAVE EARS, YOU KNOW... I DON'T NEED TO STAY HERE AND BE INSULTED."
- "FINE" "FINE"

Panel 5:
- "DO WE NEED TO RENT A CRANE?"
- "OH. I HEARD THAT. AND I AM SO OUT OF HERE."
- "MORE COFFEE?"
- "SURE."

I have subtly shown a female's butt crack in the third panel. Yet another proud milestone in my glorious career.

Panel row 1:

- "YO, DUDE, WHAT ARE YOU DOING HERE?"
- "I TOLD PIG I HAD SOME GREAT NEWS ABOUT A COUSIN OF MINE GETTING MARRIED, AND HE SAID TO COME OVER 'CAUSE HE HAD SOME GREATER NEWS."
- "YEAH. I GOT A NEW ONE."
- "GRATES ON YOU, DOESN'T HE?"
- "GOING HOME NOW."
- "STAY! SHRED SOME CHEESE!"

I draw the bush so I don't have to draw the porch. Because porches require a knowledge of perspective. And bushes, well, they're just bushes.

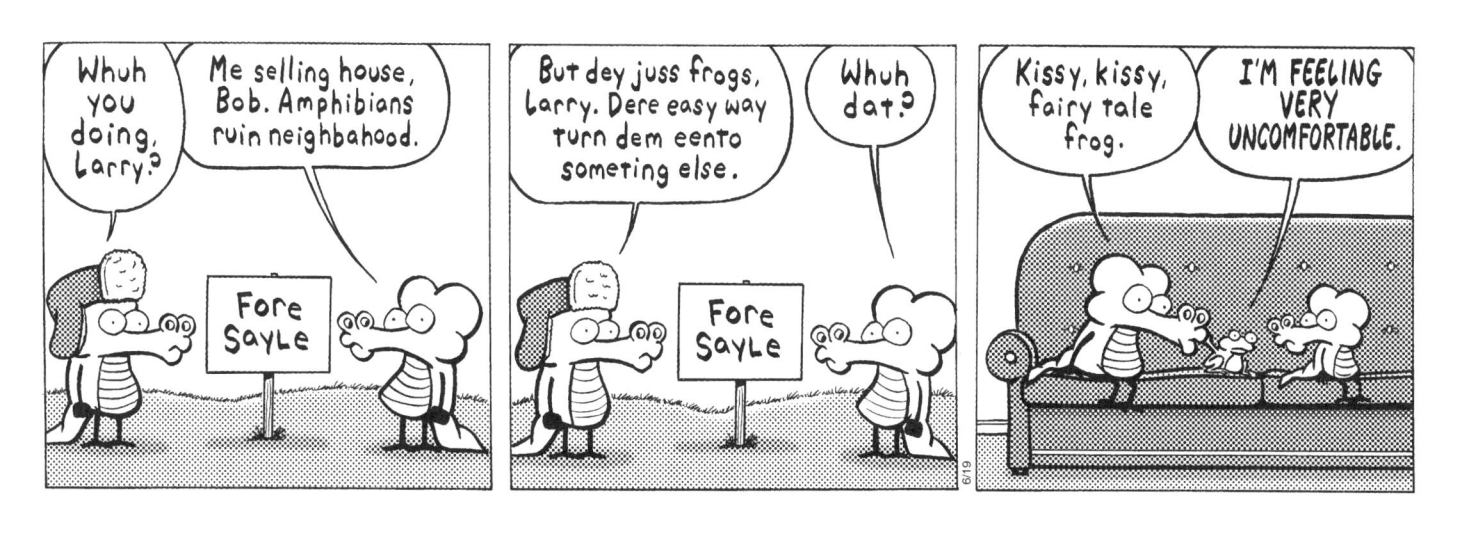

Panel row 2:

- "Whuh you doing, Larry?"
- "Me selling house, Bob. Amphibians ruin neighbahood."
- "But dey juss frogs, Larry. Dere easy way turn dem eento somering else."
- "Whuh dat?"
- "Kissy, kissy, fairy tale frog."
- "I'M FEELING VERY UNCOMFORTABLE."

Panel row 3:

- "DAD! WHY ARE YOU TRYING TO KISS FREDDY?!"
- "BOB SAY IN FAIRY TALE IT MAKE FROGS BECOME BOOT-IFUL PRINCESS!"
- "THAT'S NOT HOW THE FAIRY TALE GOES, DAD! AND WHY WOULD YOU WANT A BEAUT-IFUL PRINCESS ANYWAYS?... WHAT'S WRONG WITH MOM?"
- "Has you seen new haircut?"
- "WHAT'S THAT YOU SAY, LARRY?"
- "AHH!"
- "ME LOVE BAD NEW HAIR!"
- "ME LOVE BAD NEW HAIR!"

For the bachelors among you, "Me love bad new hair" is a guaranteed winner with the ladies.

Panel row 1:

- "DO YOU THINK IF WE'RE BAD IN LIFE, WE REALLY GO TO A PLACE CALLED 'HELL'? AND IF SO, WHAT'S IT LIKE?"
- "HELL IS A SMALL, WINDOWLESS ROOM FILLED WITH NOTHING BUT THE SOUND OF POLKA MUSIC."
- "I WILL REPENT RIGHT NOW!" "REMEMBER... ONLY SATAN COULD HAVE INVENTED THE ACCORDION."

Believe it or not, my criticism of polka music drew a very angry letter from a large polka organization. Yes, even polka has an organization. The letter ended with this plea: "We ask that you refrain from any further insulting references about polka music in your comic strip. A public apology would go a long way."

Panel row 2:

- "Dere is frog. You sure if me kees, he become bootiful princess?" "ME SURE. ME SURE. KEES NOW."
- SMOOOOOCH
- "We got probbum, Bob." "BEHOLD, THOUGHT PRINCE VALIANT, AN UGLY DRAGON TO SLAY."

I draw an awesome Prince Valiant. And when I say "draw," I mean "trace."

Panel row 3:

- "WHERE'S RAT TODAY?" "PRACTICING HIS SKI JUMP POSE. HE'S GONNA USE IT WHENEVER SOMEONE BORES HIM, AS IF TO SAY, 'I'M LEAPING RIGHT OVER YOUR TIRESOME CONVERSATION.'"
- "THAT'S RIDICULOUS. WHY DOES THE GUY HAVE TO BE SUCH A WEIRDO? WHY CAN'T HE JUST BE NORMAL NOW AND THEN?"

A strip that confuses even me. The correct order of the panels is (6), (1), (3), (5), (8), (2), (4), (7). Though I'm not entirely sure.

Okay, this has nothing to do with this strip, but I am currently writing these comments in a cafe, and the person sitting next to me is either a very old lady or Steven Tyler of Aerosmith.

Regarding that last comment, it was just an old lady.

"He said what??"

For the record, I actually think *The Family Circus* mom looks hot. Too bad she's weighed down by all those annoying children.

I believe I've said this before, but "fanny" has a whole different meaning in Great Britain. And please don't try to Google it. I don't want to be responsible for corrupting you more than I already have.

215

When I was a little kid, I invented a machine that would help me clean my room. It was a cardboard box with a bunch of long rods sticking out of it. You would grab one end of the rod, and the other end would pick things up off the floor. Had I ever actually built this brilliant invention, it would have tripled the amount of time it took me to clean my room.

Panel 1:
- HOW COME EVERYONE WHO DOES A 'LISTENER COMMENTARY' ON N.P.R. SOUNDS LIKE A SNOOTY ELITIST THAT NEEDS TO BE PUNCHED IN THE HEAD?
- WHAT ARE YOU TALKING ABOUT? THOSE ARE SMART, THOUGHTFUL PEOPLE. IN FACT, I DID ONE OF THOSE ONCE.

Panel 2:
CRACK

Panel 3:
- I'M GUESSING IT WAS SNOOTY.

Rat's feelings are mine here. Every morning I drive my son Thomas to school, and we sometimes listen to NPR. When the "Listener Commentary" comes on, I spend the entire time mocking the person giving the commentary by repeating what he or she says in a high-pitched voice.

Panel 4:
- HEY, GOAT, WHAT ARE YOU DOING?
- JUST DRINKING SOME WINE AND LISTENING TO A PODCAST OF TERRY GROSS' 'FRESH AIR'...IT'S TERRIFIC.

Panel 5:
- AH, MORE N.P.R.... I'D LIKE TO LISTEN, BUT I'M NOT AS SPECIAL AS YOU.
- OH, WILL YOU GET OFF ALL THIS 'ELITIST' CRAP? N.P.R.'S A GREAT STATION THAT COVERS EVERYTHING...*EVERYTHING.*

Panel 6:
- MONSTER TRUCK RALLIES?

Panel 7:
- OKAY, THERE ARE LIMITS.
- HAVE A BEER. WE COMMONERS ENJOY IT.

Shortly after this ran, a person on NPR's web site pointed out that I was wrong. NPR had indeed done a recent story on monster truck rallies. Stupid elitists.

Panel 8:
- GOSH, THIS BOOK ON CHARLES DARWIN IS GREAT... IT GETS PAST ALL THE CONTROVERSY SURROUNDING HIS THEORY OF NATURAL SELECTION AND JUST EXPLAINS IT.
- WHAT'S NATURAL SELECTION?

Panel 9:
- IT'S WHEN A MAN CHOOSES TO BE WITH A WOMAN WHO DOES NOT HAVE SURGICALLY ENHANCED TA-TAS.

Panel 10:
- NO WONDER IT'S CONTROVERSIAL.
- IT'S A VERY TOUGH CHOICE.
- STOP!!

Panel 1:
- "WHAT ARE YOU DOING, RAT?"
- "I HAVE MOVED TO AN ISLAND."

Panel 2:
- "WHAT FOR?"
- "TO FOREVER SEPARATE MYSELF FROM THIS WORLD THAT I HATE. SO GOODBYE, GOOD FRIEND, UNTIL WE MEET AGAIN IN A BETTER PLACE."

Panel 3:
- "STUPID TIDE."

This was supposed to be the start of a long series, but the palm tree took too long to draw, so I made it a very short series.

Panel 4:
- "EXCUSE ME, EVERYONE...I HAVE AN ANNOUNCEMENT TO MAKE...I JUST GOT BACK FROM THAT NEW CAFE DOWNTOWN. THEY HAD THREE DIFFERENT SIZES OF COFFEE CUPS. AND THEY HAD LIDS."
- "SO WHAT, PIG?.. EVERY COFFEE PLACE HAS LIDS."

Panel 5:
- "THE SAME LID FIT ALL THREE CUPS!!"

Panel 6:
- "THIS IS WHY WE SHOULD LOCK HIM IN HIS ROOM."
- "HAS THE NOBEL PRIZE EVER BEEN SUCH A LOCK?!"

Story update: As it turns out, the lid inventor was *not* awarded the Nobel Prize.

Panel 7:
- "DO YOU THINK EACH OF US HAS FREE WILL?"
- "NO. ONLY SOME OF US."

Panel 8:
- "WHY DO YOU SAY THAT?"
- "BECAUSE NOT EVERYONE BOUGHT THE DVD."

Panel 9:
- "FREE WILL, NOT 'FREE WILLY.'"
- "OH, GREAT. IS THAT SOME BORING RE-MAKE?"

I need to start making movie references that are not twenty years old.

I deserve a way better epitaph.

I didn't quite know what to do with Dinky Duckling, so I thought I'd connect him to Guard Duck. But it wasn't that productive of a story line. So like Dinky's mother, I would soon abandon Dinky as a character.

I really like Rat's line in the last panel. I'd be a lot more humble about writing it if I had a reason to be.

I was not on drugs when I drew this.

Panel 1: HEY THERE, GOAT... COME WATCH TV WITH US.

Panel 2: NO THANKS. I HAVE A BOOK TO READ. / WHAT BOOK?

Panel 3: IT'S ON NATURAL SELECTION. IT EXPLAINS HOW A CHANGE THAT BETTER EQUIPS AN ANIMAL TO LIVE GETS PASSED ON TO ITS DESCENDANTS, THEREBY ALTERING THE SPECIES FOREVER.

Panel 4: I'M SORRY...DO YOU UNDERSTAND WHAT THAT MEANS?

Panel 5: THAT MY KIDS WILL HAVE PILLOWS FOR BUTTS.

Panel 6: NO. / AND A REMOTE CONTROL FOR A HAND? / AND CHEESE POOFS FOR FEET?!

If you look around at people in your daily life, you'll see that a lot of them really do have large pillows for butts.

Strip 1:

"Okay, zeeba neighba... Me and Frank decide go downtown, act een community play. Frank tink it help us take mind off pressure of being predator."

"OH, YEAH? WELL, KNOCK 'EM DEAD."

CRACK

"How dat help play?"

Approximate croc death count: 636.

Strip 2:

LARRY TRIES OUT FOR COMMUNITY THEATER

"WELL, HELLO, SIR... ARE YOU HERE TO VOLUNTEER FOR OUR COMMUNITY PLAY?"

"Yeah. Me want role where me, like, domeenate... You know, like, keel lot peeple, eet guy's hed."

"I TAKE IT YOU'VE NEVER SEEN 'MARY POPPINS'."

"No. How high body count?"

Strip 3:

"HEY, NEIGHBOR BOB. CHECK OUT THIS BOOK. IT'S ABOUT COMPANY TOWNS AT THE TURN OF THE CENTURY. THESE POOR WORKERS LIVED EVERY FREE MOMENT OF THEIR LIVES IN THE SHADOW OF THEIR EVER-PRESENT EMPLOYER."

"HOW AWFUL. WHY DID THEY PUT UP WITH—"

Ding

"Hey, Bob, I know it's your day off, but Jeff needs that report *ASAP*."

"I GOTTA GO."

Oooh. Social commentary. Is there anything I can't do?

DID DAD GET THE ROLE HE TRIED OUT FOR IN THE COMMUNITY PLAY? / **OF COURSE NOT. IT WAS 'MARY POPPINS.'**	**SO THAT'S WHERE HE GOT THE IDEA.** / **WHAT IDEA?**	Me gonna fly over hedge, zeeba neighba! / **GO FOR IT.**

DAD'S ON THE ROOF DRESSED AS MARY POPPINS. I THINK HE WANTS TO FLY INTO ZEBRA'S YARD. / **PLEASE, SON... EVEN YOUR IDIOT DAD KNOWS MARY POPPINS COULDN'T REALLY FLY.**	SupercalifrAAAAHHHHHHH	**CLOSE THE DRAPES, SON.** / Chim Chiminy @☆⊙#

After I drew this Mary "Larry" Poppins strip, I realized I had made a big mistake. I had failed to draw Larry as Mary Poppins. So I had to go back and redraw the second panel. Cartooning tip: If you're going to draw a Larry-as-Mary-Poppins series, try to remember to draw Larry as Mary Poppins.

Hey, Rat...Didja see the funny YouTube video me and Goat emailed you?	I did. TOO LOL.	**TOO LOL?**	The Opposite Of Laugh Out Loud	**THAT HURTS.**

Please. Help me make this acronym catch on.

Danny Donkey went to the park.

A woman approached him.

HELP SAVE OUR TRAIN, SIR. IT'S FOR THE CHILDREN.

Danny Donkey looked up and saw a miniature steam train in disrepair.

"I will save your train," said Danny Donkey. "And give it a new and shiny track."

YAY

So Danny Donkey spent all his money and fixed the train.

And on the day of the re-opening, everyone cheered the shiny new train.

And watched as it departed the new station and rolled down its shiny new track.

Which now led out of the park.

And straight to the liquor store.

"'I HAVE BUILT THE WORLD'S MOST CONVENIENT BEER RUN,' SHOUTED DANNY."

THIS IS YOUR COMMEMORATION OF NEIGHBORHOOD IMPROVEMENT DAY?

NO CHILD SHALL EVER BE THIRSTY AGAIN!!

This got complaints. But that's okay, because it made me laugh.

Panel strip 1:

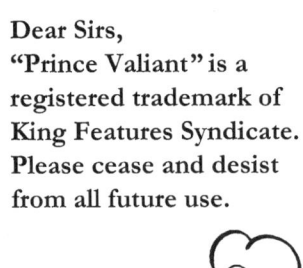

- "HEY, RAT, YOU GONNA HELP ME CLEAN OUT MY GARAGE NEXT WEEK?" "WHY SHOULD I?"
- "WELL, FIRST OFF—"
- CRACK
- "'FIRST OFF' IS NEVER FOLLOWED BY ANYTHING GOOD."

Panel strip 2:

- "DAD! DAD! YOU BROUGHT BACK FREDDY THE FROG! HE'S NO LONGER PRINCE VALIANT!" "Oh, dat?... Yeah.. Me trying be more open-mind 'bout amfibians."
- "THAT'S GREAT, DAD...WHAT'S THAT IN YOUR HAND?" "Oh, dis? Dis nutting. You no need read or—"
- Dear Sirs, "Prince Valiant" is a registered trademark of King Features Syndicate. Please cease and desist from all future use.
- "OPEN-MINDED?" "Lawyer-minded. Doze guys ruin everyting."

I did not actually get a "cease and desist" letter. But I did get tired of drawing Prince Valiant. And thus, he disappeared.

Panel strip 3:

- "HEY, SIR, WHEN I WAS WITH MOM, SHE FED ME THREE TIMES A DAY, PLANNED OUT ALL MY MEALS, MADE SURE I GOT ALL THE DIFFERENT FOOD GROUPS...HOW ARE WE GONNA HANDLE THAT?"
- "HERE'S A TWINKIE. MAKE IT LAST."
- "THIS IS WAY MORE FUN." "NEED A COLD ONE TO WASH IT DOWN?"

Panel 1 (strip 1):
- "HEY, RAT. WHATCHA GETTING FOR BREAKFAST?"
- "I'M THINKING ABOUT ORDERING A BUNCH OF BACTERIA THAT'S BEEN THROWN INTO MILK AND ALLOWED TO FERMENT."
- "IT'S CALLED YOGURT."
- "I LIKE TO BE PRECISE."

This really is what yogurt is. So please, all you health-conscious people, start eating bacon and eggs like the rest of us.

Panel 2 (strip 2):
- "HEY, GOAT. WHAT DO YOU WANT TO DRINK?"
- "BREAK DOWN SOME GRAIN IN HOT WATER AND LET A BUNCH OF FUNGI EAT IT AND THEN GIVE ME THEIR WASTE PRODUCTS."
- "IT'S CALLED *BEER*, ⊙☆#⊙ IT!!"
- "I LIKE TO BE PRECISE."

I recently took a tour of a large brewery in Boston. When I heard about this part of the brewing process, I decided to never again try to learn anything about what I eat or drink.

Panel 3 (strip 3):
- "DO YOU REALIZE THAT HALF OF THIS COUNTRY PRONOUNCES THE WORD 'AUNT' *ANT*, WHILE THE OTHER HALF PRONOUNCES IT *AWNT*?"
- "CAN'T WE ALL JUST GET ALONG??!"
- "HE'S VERY SENSITIVE TO DIVISION."
- "PIG, THEY'RE NOT SHOOTING EACH OTHER."
- "JOIN MY CANDLELIGHT VIGIL FOR PEACE, WON'T YOU?"

As a Californian, I am firmly in the "ant" camp.

WHERE ARE YOU, RAT? YOU PROMISED TO HELP PIG AND ME CLEAN OUT MY GARAGE.
I'M LYING ON MY @#@ WITH A BEER ON MY BELLY.
WHY??
NASA.
NASA?
NASA ISSUED A REPORT SAYING THERE ARE CURRENTLY 47,000 ASTEROIDS THAT ARE BIG ENOUGH AND CLOSE ENOUGH TO POSE A THREAT TO EARTH.
SO?!
SO EVERYTHING'S POINTLESS. GOODBYE.
SO YOU'RE GONNA LEAVE THE ENTIRE JOB TO ME AND—
HE'S CLEARLY LOST ALL PERSPECTIVE.

Panel 1:
- HEY, JEFF THE CYCLIST... DO YOU PRAY? SOME PEOPLE THINK IT HELPS TO KEEP A GUY HUMBLE.
- I DO, AS A MATTER OF FACT.

Panel 2:
- THAT'S GREAT. WHO DO YOU PRAY TO?
- MYSELF, FOR I AM A GOD ON THIS EARTH.

Panel 3:
- CYCLISTS ARE A UNIQUE BUNCH.
- LEMME GUESS... FATTY McFAT FAT WANTS TO PRAY TO ME.

Around this time, some readers began questioning whether Jeff the Cyclist was a reference to comic strip creator Jef Mallett. Jef draws the comic strip *Frazz* and is an avid cyclist. I didn't intend that, but knowing that people were looking for signs, I wrote part of the word "Frazz" on Jeff's left sleeve.

Panel 1:
- HEY, STEPH, WHAT'S IT TAKE TO BE A SYNDICATED CARTOONIST? IS IT BEING A GOOD WRITER? KNOWING A LOT OF JOKES? HAVING THE RIGHT PEN?
- WELL, PIG, YOU HAVE TO—

Panel 2:
- ...BE A LONELY NERD IN HIGH SCHOOL WHO SPENT ALL HIS TIME DRAWING BECAUSE HE HAD NO FRIENDS AND COULDN'T ATTRACT GIRLS.

Panel 3:
- WE DO HAVE FEELINGS, YOU KNOW.
- FEELINGS, SURE. IT'S DATES YOU COULDN'T GET.

This really was true about my high school days. I can admit that now because I have matured into a towering stud of a man.

Panel 1:
- WELL, GUYS, I'M OFF. TODAY IS MY FAMILY'S ANNUAL POTATO SACK RACE. IT'S SORT OF A TRADITION.
- WHAT'S 'TRADITION'?

Panel 2:
- TRADITION IS THE REASON FOR DOING SOMETHING YOU CAN NO LONGER THINK OF A REASON FOR DOING.

Panel 3:
- I HATE IT WHEN I AGREE WITH YOU.
- SO THAT'S WHY WE STILL SEE OUR ANNOYING FAMILY.

Strip 1:
- "Hey, Mom, why did you cut your hair?"
- "To express myself better."
- "What do you mean?"
- "Well, sweetie, pretend for a moment that I wanted to tell you the secret of a successful life, but I have my old hair."
- "Okay."
- "Okay... the secret of a successful life is"
- "Speech balloon interference."
- "The curse of the big-haired woman."

The secret of a successful life is not changing a character's hairstyle, because in future strips it will confuse the creator and he will not be able to remember what color it is.

Strip 2:
- "Hi, Mom... it's me, Pig... I'm tired of you controlling my life, so I'm gonna go outside and declare my independence from you in a voice the whole world can hear."
- "She said to put on a jacket."

Strip 3:
- "Hey, Goat, want to see an animated movie with me and Rat?"
- "I guess. But why's Rat carrying a book of Russian plays?"
- "Because all animated movies have sickeningly sweet endings. And all Russian plays end with someone shooting themselves. So when the film nears its saccharine end, I just stand and read the last page of the play aloud, thereby keeping the whole universe in balance."
- "Oh, that must be heartwarming."
- "It is? Then listen to this... 'And Ivan shot himself. The end.'"
- "Awww... poor l'il Ivan."

This arose out of a series of Anton Chekhov plays that I read. In almost every single one, the main character kills himself on the last page. I'm telling you, compared to Russian plays, *Pearls Before Swine* is a wonderful place filled with puppies and rainbows.

"YOU ENJOYING THE COAST, PIGITA?" "NOT REALLY."	"I THOUGHT YOU LIKED IT HERE." "I DO. AND I LIKE STARING OUT AT THE BOATS. I THINK IT'S JUST THE SAND IN MY TOES I DON'T LIKE."
"OH." "I'M SORRY. I'M JUST NOT A BEACHY KIND OF GIRL."	"WOULD YOU RATHER WALK AROUND THE PORT?" "OH, I LOVE PORTS."
"SO YOU'RE MORE OF A PORTLY KIND OF GIRL."	"MAYBE WE SHOULD AVOID THE COAST ENTIRELY."

Why do my characters wear bathing suits at the beach when they wear nothing at all in everyday life? If you know, please let me know, so I can look intelligent the next time someone asks.

Pearls often gets shrunk down tremendously in newspapers. So there's a good chance this was not even readable in some newspapers.

The vast majority of random humans in Pearls are bald. That's because it's easier than drawing hair.

232

Panel row 1:

- "WOW. LOOK AT THAT WOMAN'S GREAT JUGS."
- "PIG, THAT'S RIDICULOUSLY INAPPROPRIATE. GO SAY YOU'RE SORRY."
- "SORRY."
- "FOR WHAT?" "I DON'T KNOW." "I GIVE UP."

I was rather surprised I got away with this.

Panel row 2:

- "HEY, RAT, IF YOU'RE GONNA COME OVER AND EAT MY CHIPS, PUT THIS BAG CLIP ON THEM WHEN YOU'RE DONE SO THE CHIPS STAY FRESH." "CONSIDER IT DONE."
- "GREAT. SO YOU'LL DO IT?" "NO. I JUST WANT YOU TO CONSIDER IT DONE SO YOU'LL STOP WHINING LIKE AN OVERSENSITIVE NINNY."
- "GIVE 'EM BACK." "CONSIDER IT DONE."

Panel row 3:

- "WHAT DOES IT MEAN WHEN PEOPLE SAY THINGS AREN'T WHAT THEY APPEAR TO BE?" "WELL, TAKE THAT GIRL OVER THERE."
- "WHAT ABOUT HER?" "SHE APPEARS TO BE LISTENING TO MUSIC ON HER iPOD. BUT SHE'S NOT. SHE JUST KEEPS THOSE EARBUDS IN HER EARS TO KEEP LOSERS SHE DOESN'T WANT TO TALK TO FROM TALKING TO HER."
- "OHHH, THAT'S NOT TRUE, IS—" "♪LA LA LA LALALAA LISTENING TO MUSIC...CAN'T HEAR ANYTHING..."

I need to start drawing women bald as well. That would be a big time-saver.

233

This angered the polka crowd all over again. One reader of the Syracuse *Post-Standard* called the strip "ignorant, nasty, degrading and anti-Polish." So if you're still keeping score at home, the most humorless people in the world are: 1) radical Turks; 2) cyclists in tight pants; and 3) polka lovers.

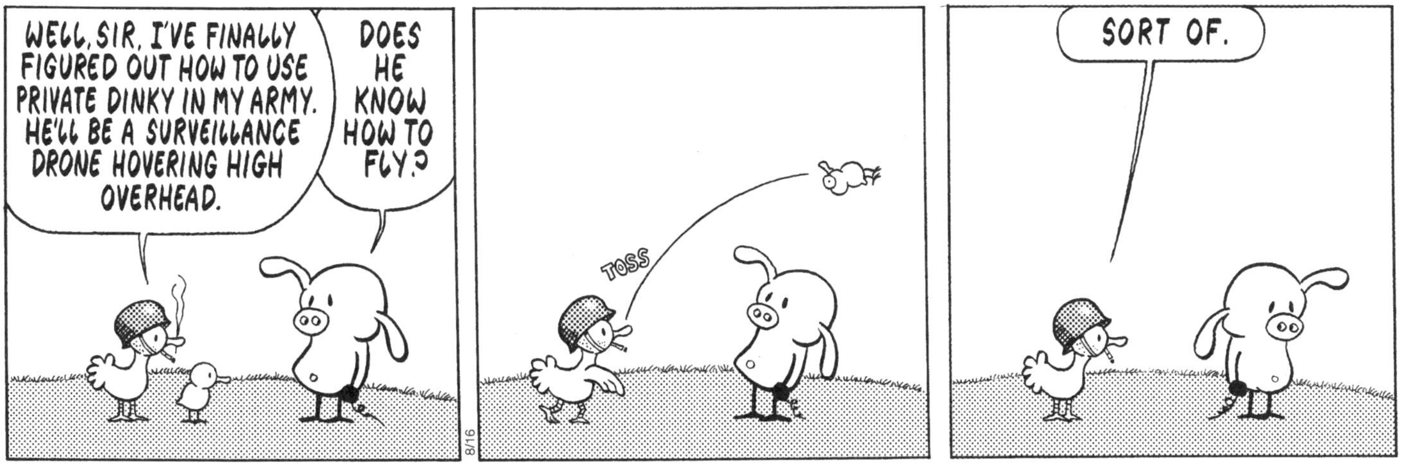
WELL, SIR, I'VE FINALLY FIGURED OUT HOW TO USE PRIVATE DINKY IN MY ARMY. HE'LL BE A SURVEILLANCE DRONE HOVERING HIGH OVERHEAD.
DOES HE KNOW HOW TO FLY?
8/16
TOSS
SORT OF.

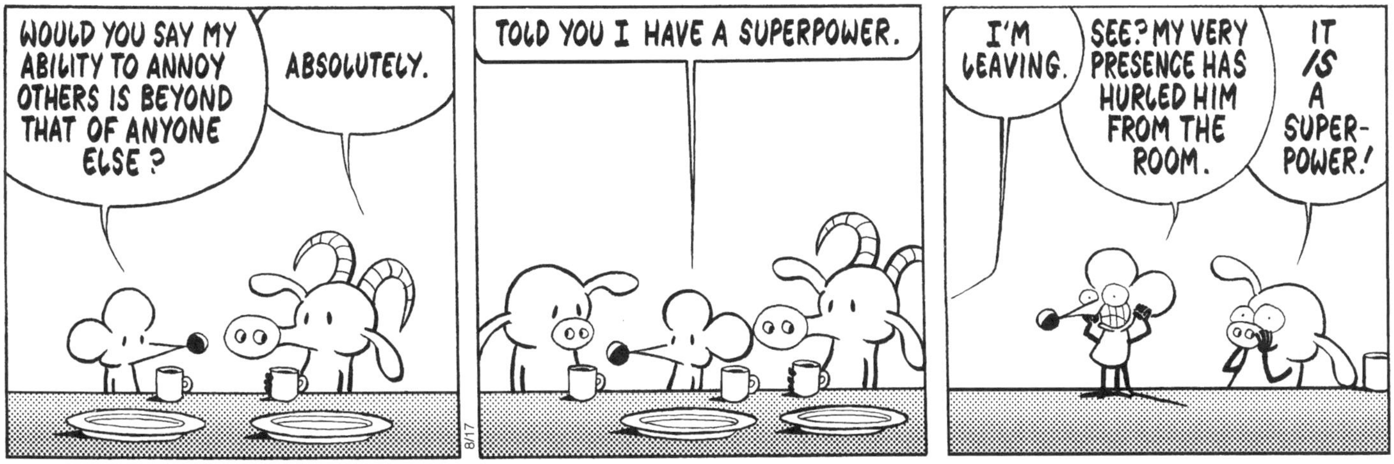
WOULD YOU SAY MY ABILITY TO ANNOY OTHERS IS BEYOND THAT OF ANYONE ELSE?
ABSOLUTELY.
TOLD YOU I HAVE A SUPERPOWER.
8/17
I'M LEAVING.
SEE? MY VERY PRESENCE HAS HURLED HIM FROM THE ROOM.
IT *IS* A SUPER-POWER!

I have this super power.

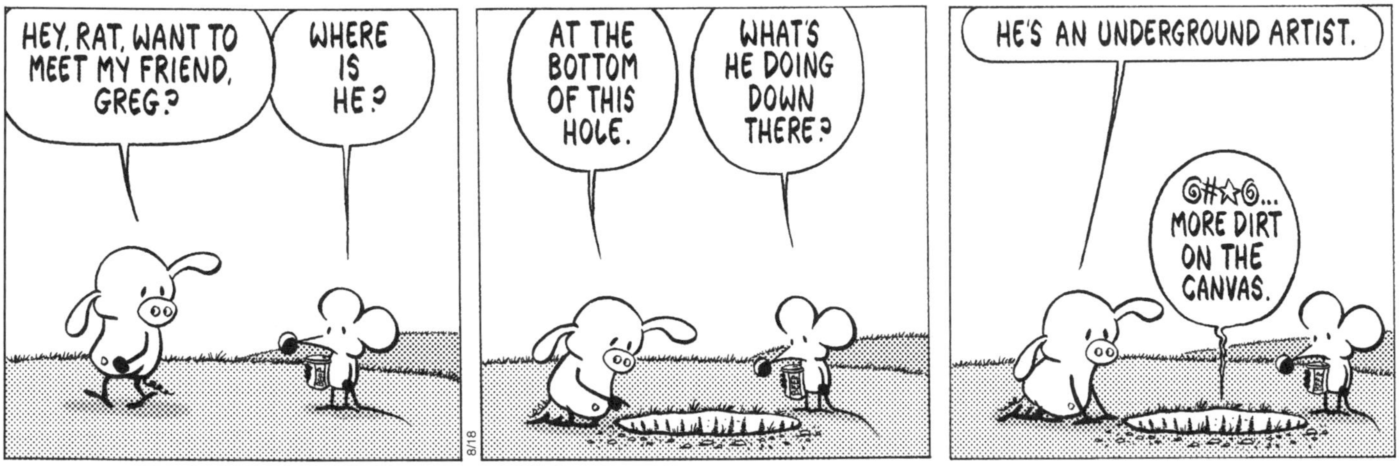
HEY, RAT, WANT TO MEET MY FRIEND, GREG?
WHERE IS HE?
AT THE BOTTOM OF THIS HOLE.
WHAT'S HE DOING DOWN THERE?
8/18
HE'S AN UNDERGROUND ARTIST.
@#☆@... MORE DIRT ON THE CANVAS.

This joke arose out of a book signing. Somebody asked me if I got many complaints about the amount of violence in the strip and what I thought about those complaints. I said I didn't understand the complaints because as a kid I had watched lots of violent Bugs Bunny cartoons and yet still turned out okay. As soon as I said I had turned out okay, people started giggling. That's when I realized I should never again cite myself as an example of normalcy.

Panel strip 1:
- "PIG, I'VE MADE A CHOICE... ...ABOUT US. I WOULD LIKE TO BE...UH...IN A WORD... WELL...I'LL JUST SAY IT... CELIBATE!"
- "YAY! YAY!"
- "YOU'RE FINE WITH THAT?" "FINE? I LOVE TO CELEBRATE."
- "LET'S START OVER." "WHY? JOIN IN!" *TOOOOOOT*

I teach kids a lot of new words. I should win some educational award for that.

Panel strip 2:
- "HEY, GUYS, WHAT ARE YOU DOING?" "PLAYING 'TRIVIAL PURSUIT' AGAINST JIMMY THE JELLYFISH."
- "WHY ARE YOU PLAYING AGAINST JIMMY?" "BECAUSE JELLYFISH HAVE NO BRAIN."
- "WHAT'S THE CAPITAL OF TEXAS?" "BLUE." "AWW, TOO BAD, JIMMY, YOU LOSE AGAIN."

I would be really, really good at the original *Trivial Pursuit* if it were not for the Entertainment category. It is filled with stupid questions about stupid topics like stupid TV shows and stupid movies. And if it sounds like I'm bitter, I am.

Panel strip 3:
- "I MISS MY MOTHER." "YOU'LL BE OKAY, PRIVATE. YOU'RE A SURVEILLANCE DRONE NOW."
- "HOW DOES THAT HELP?" "BECAUSE YOU'RE GONNA SHOW EVERYONE WHO EVER REJECTED YOU HOW GREAT YOU'VE BECOME, HOW IMPORTANT, HOW WORLDLY...HOW..."
- *Toss*
- "SOMETIMES IT'S EASIER TO JUST DEMONSTRATE."

And just like that, Dinky the character was gone. Literally and figuratively tossed out of the strip.

Hey, look, a big scene filled with random humans, and only two of them are bald. That's artistic progress.

Strip 1 (8/23):

Pig: HEY, RAT, WHAT'S THAT?
Rat: MY NEW INVENTION, THE 'TROUBLE BOX.' IF YOU HAVE TROUBLES, YOU PUT 'EM IN HERE AND THEY'RE GONE FOREVER. GO AHEAD, PUT A COUPLE IN THERE.

Pig (writing): I'm dumb and need affection.

Rat: Hee Hee Hee Hee

Rat: FIRST I LAUGH AT THEM.

Strip 2 (8/24):

Rat: YOU EVER NOTICE HOW WE SEE MUCH OF LIFE THROUGH THE PRISM OF OURSELVES?
Goat: HOW SO?

Rat: WHEN PEOPLE AROUND US DO THINGS, WE ASSUME THEIR MOTIVATION FOR DOING SO MUST HAVE SOMETHING TO DO WITH OURSELVES, WHEN IN TRUTH MOST DECISIONS HAVE NOTHING TO DO WITH US.
Goat: THAT'S INTERESTING, BUT I NEED TO GET GOING.

Rat: WHY? BECAUSE I'M BORING?

Goat: BECAUSE I'LL MISS MY DENTIST APPOINTMENT.
Rat: CALL ME 'BORING' AGAIN. I DARE YOU.

Goat should really stay out of that cafe. Nothing good ever happens there.

Strip 3 (8/25):

Rat: Hey, zeeba. You like cooking wid gas or charcoal?
Zebra: WELL, THAT'S THE GREAT DEBATE, ISN'T IT? BUT I SUPPOSE I'D HAVE TO SAY CHARCOAL.

Rat: Gud. Geet on grill.

Rat: Guy never cooperate.

People really do fight over this. If you don't believe me, Google "gas versus charcoal debate." If nothing else, it will prove to you that some people have way too much time on their hands.

Dude, Have Guard Duck destroy Pakistan.	Rat should get wasted at Disneyland and punch people in the face!!	Do one where a girl takes off her bikini top. Says, "Glad to get that off my chest."

PLEASE PLEASE PLEASE do something with Star Wars where everyone blows up. **STAR WARS ROCKS!!!!!!**	My wife Jessica's 39th birthday is on Friday. Have your strip that day say, "Happy B-Day, Jess!"	MORE CROCS!!!	Less crocs.

KILL ALL YOUR CHARACTERS P.S. Please give me credit if you use this idea.	HEY, STEPH, I HAD AN IDEA FOR A STRIP... DO YOU TAKE SUGGESTIONS? — NO. — SO *THIS* IS WHERE YOU GET YOUR IDEAS.

Most of these are actual suggestions that have been sent to me.

Panel 1 (8/27):
- Pig: HEY, GOAT, I WAS GONNA ASK YOU TO STAY FOR DINNER, BUT THAT HOMEMADE PASTA I GOT FROM PROFESSOR LUNDQUIST WENT STALE.
- Goat: IS HE THAT PROFESSOR OF LANGUAGE DOWN AT THE COLLEGE?
- Pig: YEAH. HE GAVE ME ALL THIS LINGUINE THAT I JUST LET SIT OPEN ON THE SHELF. I FEEL ABSOLUTELY TERRIBLE ABOUT IT.
- Goat: SO YOU HAVE LINGUIST LUNDQUIST'S LINGUINE LANGUISH ANGUISH?
- Pig: I HATE THAT GUY.

It's sad when even Goat starts ripping on me.

Panel 2 (8/28):
- Goat: WHERE'S PIG TODAY?
- Rat: GETTING READY FOR A DATE WITH A GIRL HE KNEW YEARS AGO. BUT HE'S WORRIED 'CAUSE HE THINKS HE'S TOO FAT NOW.
- Goat: POOR GUY. WHAT'S HE GONNA DO?
- Rat: I TOLD HIM IF HE WANTS TO LOOK THINNER, HE SHOULD WEAR SOMETHING WITH VERTICAL STRIPES.
- Pig: I FEEL BETTER NOW.

Panel 3 (8/29):
- Rat: WHAT'S WITH THIS NEW TREND WITH GUYS KEEPING THEIR SUNGLASSES ON THE BACK OF THEIR HEAD?
- Goat: YEAH. IT'S A LITTLE STRANGE, BUT WHAT ARE YOU GONNA DO ABOUT IT.
- Rat: YOU LOOK STUPID.
- Goat: THERE'S THAT.

Strip 1:

- "HEY, GOAT...I MADE A NEW FRIEND. HE'S A BOUNCER."
- "A BOUNCER, HUH? MUST BE PRETTY TOUGH."
- *BOUNCE BOUNCE BOUNCE*
- "NOT REALLY."

I thought this was really funny, but it didn't get a huge reaction. So please, if you didn't laugh, keep reading it until you do.

Strip 2:

- "Hullooo zeeba neighba. Leesten. Crocs start barber shop. Want haircut?"
- "I DON'T THINK I'D FEEL COMFORTABLE WITH YOUR BARBER."
- "Whuh wrong wid barber?"
- "Guy juss lack people skills."

I used to have a barber who would get very agitated about politics. He'd get so mad that he would almost start yelling. Then I'd start thinking, "This guy might kill me." So I switched barbers.

Strip 3:

- "HAVE YOU SEEN ALL THOSE ELECTRONIC SIGNS THE CITY PUTS BY THE SIDE OF THE ROAD TELLING YOU THE SPEED YOU'RE DRIVING?"
- "YEAH. THEY'RE TO MAKE YOU SLOW DOWN."
- "OH."
- "'OH' WHAT?"
- "I KEEP TRYING TO SET A SPEED RECORD."
- "PLEASE STOP TALKING TO ME."
- "SO THE NUMBERS ARE *NOT* SENT TO THE 'GUINNESS BOOK OF WORLD RECORDS'?"

The framed picture in the second panel is an homage to the legendary comic strip *Krazy Kat*. The reference to splitting one's pants in the last panel is an homage to my best friend, Emilio, who in grade school split his pants numerous times playing tetherball. And if humiliating your best friend isn't a great way to end a treasury, I don't know what it is.

Wading into the Kiddie Pool

The following section contains drawings I did as a kid. I found them all in a little suitcase in the attic of our current house.

Taken collectively, I believe they show that unlike Mozart, I was not born an artistic genius.

I merely blossomed into one.

Sincerely,
Stephan "Humble as Ever" Pastis

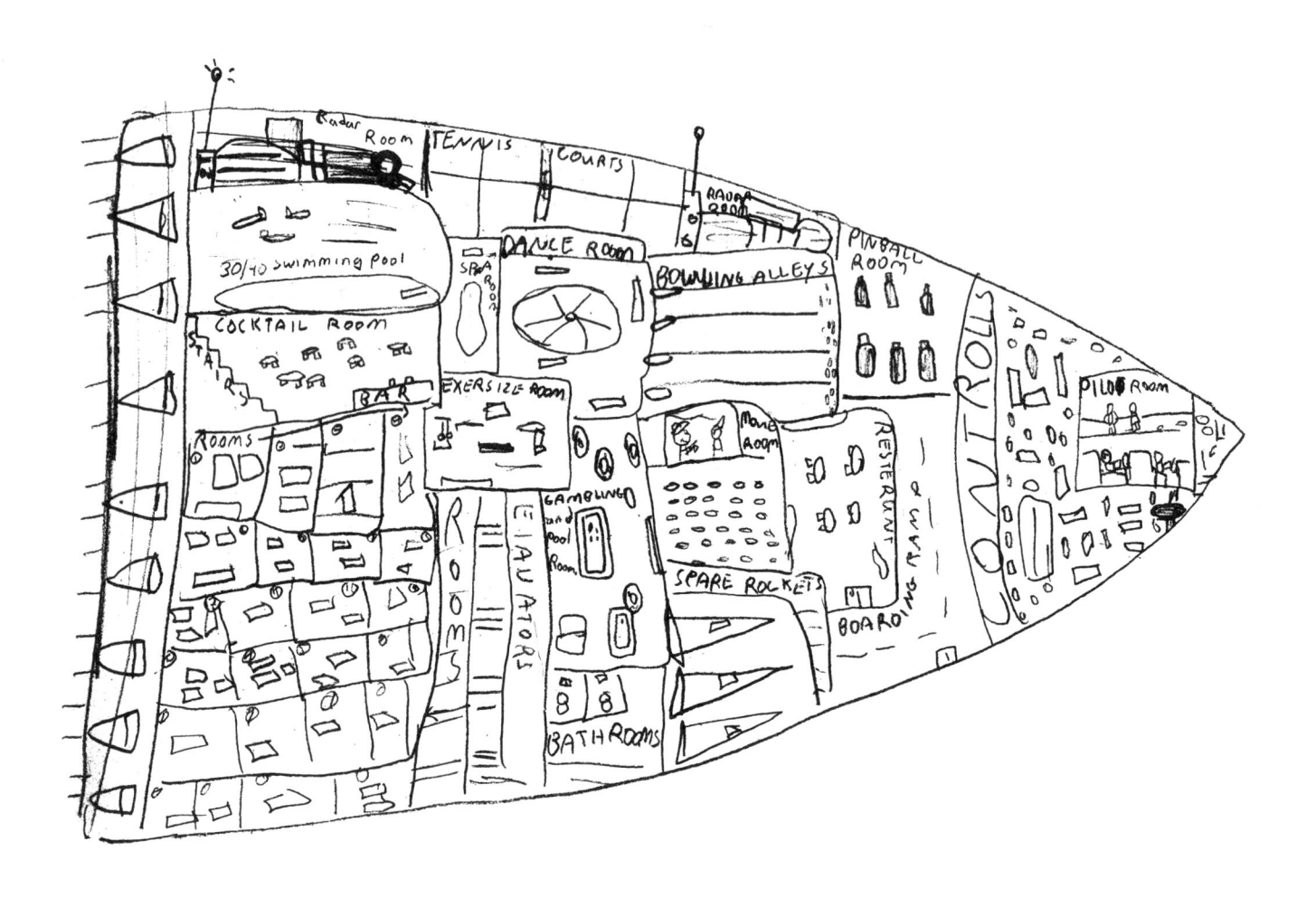

Drawing 1 — Always Thinking Ahead

This appears to be some kind of rocket ship. What I like about it is that ten-year-old me made sure to add one room for "gambling" and another for "cocktails."

Drawing 2—Just Before They Got Rubbed Out

I believe these are supposed to be my parents. And the third guy is a mobster holding them hostage. What a wonderfully sweet drawing.

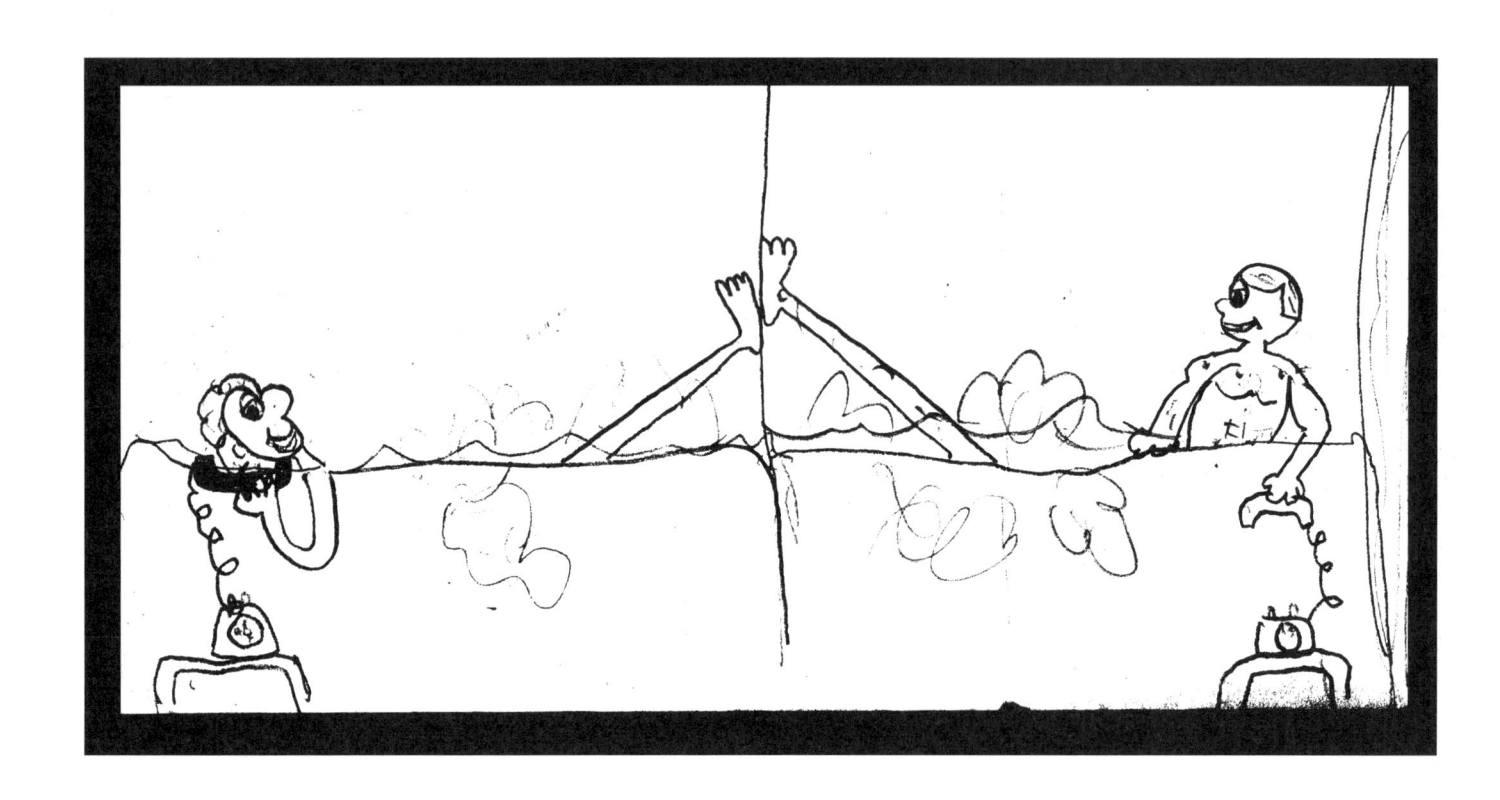

Drawing 3 — Not Appropriate for Children Under Seventeen

I don't know what *you* were drawing when you were eight,
but I was drawing nude men and women talking on the telephone.
And I'm really hoping that long thing sticking out of the man's tub is his leg.

Drawing 4 — Egging Me On

May 24, 1976. Eight-year-old Stephan tells his first pun.
And it's just about as funny as the ones he would tell three decades later.

Drawing 5—Is That a Carrot in Your Pocket?

"The Mr. Vegetable Beautty Pageant."
The point in my career where thematically, I begin to drift off the rails.

Drawing 6—Hunk of Burning Love

A compelling portrait of Elvis Presley. As if you didn't know that.

Drawing 7 — Even I Don't Know the Answer to This Question

Here we have 1) a school principal being crushed by blocks; 2) a car about to run over a classroom full of kids; and 3) the ever-cryptic question, "Where's my lamb?"

Drawing 8 — It's Not Racist, But It's Close

Kids, the single-panel comic that somehow failed to sweep the nation. In this installment, the child has dug such a deep hole that he has apparently reached China, causing the other child to say, "I think you did it. I see a fortune cookie."

Drawing 9 — It's Funny Because He's Blind

As best as I can tell, this may be the first comic strip I ever created. In the first panel, the nearsighted boy asks, "Where are my glasses?" In the second panel, he points to a zebra in a cage and says to his mother, "Mom, may I have that penguin?" So just one day into my cartooning career, and already I'm making fun of people with disabilities.

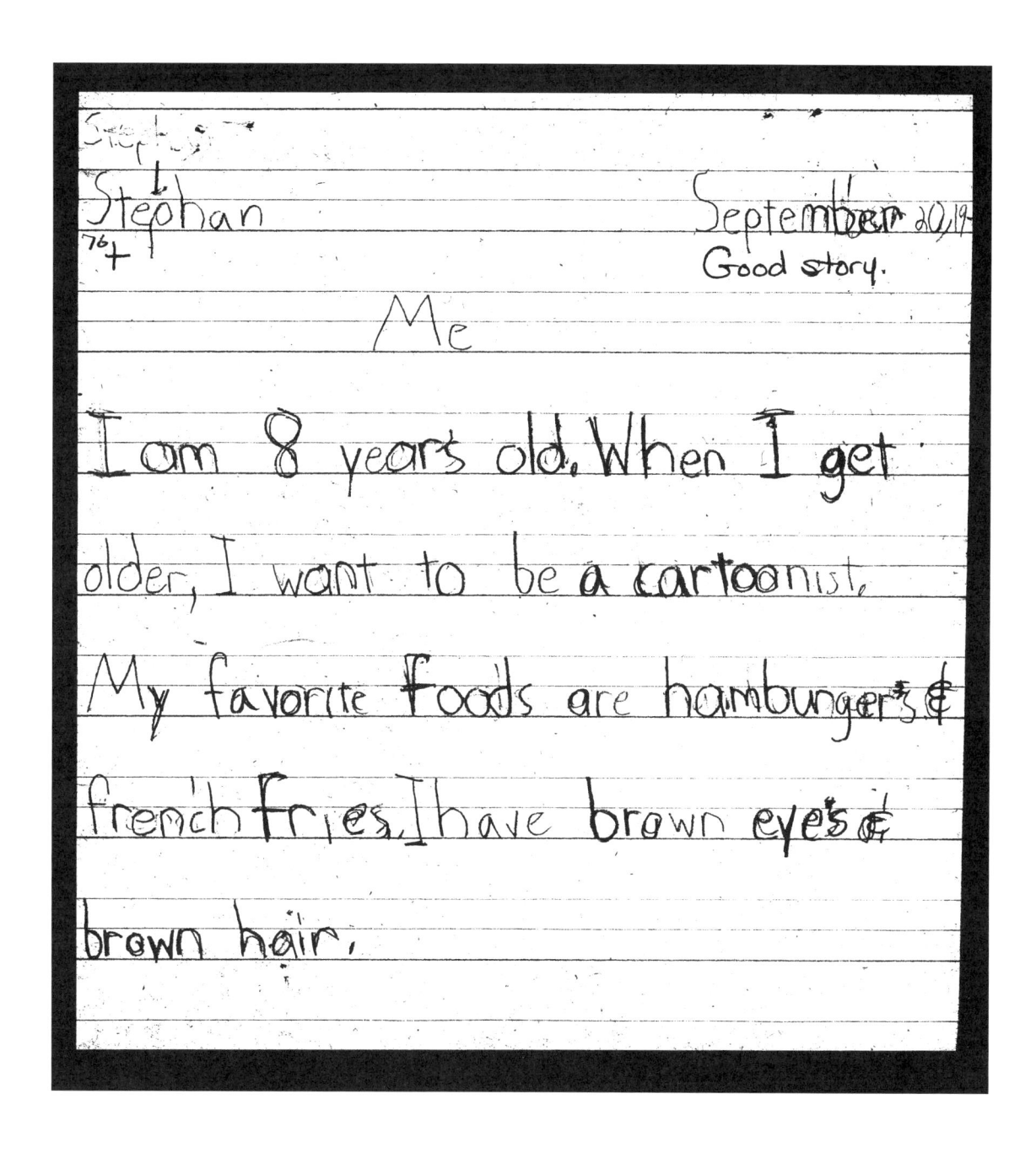

> Stephan   September 20, 19
> 76+   Good story.
>
>   Me
>
> I am 8 years old. When I get older, I want to be a cartoonist. My favorite foods are hamburgers & french fries. I have brown eyes & brown hair.

Drawing 10 — Take That, You Disbelieving Teacher

My September 20, 1976 report on me, which includes the sentence, "When I get older, I want to be a cartoonist." I like how my teacher has written "Good story" at the top of the page, as if to say, "This all sounds like fiction."